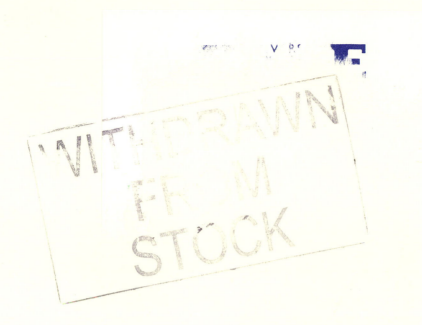

WRITING AND PSYCHOLOGY

Writing and Psychology

UNDERSTANDING WRITING AND ITS TEACHING FROM THE PERSPECTIVE OF COMPOSITION STUDIES

Douglas Vipond

PRAEGER

Westport, Connecticut
London

Library of Congress Cataloging-in-Publication Data

Vipond, Douglas.
    Writing and psychology : understanding writing and its teaching
from the perspective of composition studies / Douglas Vipond.
      p.   cm.
    Includes bibliographical references and index.
    ISBN 0–275–94637–1 (alk. paper)
    1. Psychology—Authorship. 2. Rhetoric and psychology.
3. Psychological literature. 4. English language—Rhetoric—Study
and teaching. 5. Publication manual of the American Psychological
Association. I. Title.
BF76.8.V56   1994
808′.001′9—dc20   93–15815

British Library Cataloguing in Publication Data is available.

Library of Congress Catalog Card Number: 93–15815
ISBN: 0–275–94637–1

First published in 1993

Praeger Publishers, 88 Post Road West, Westport, CT 06881
An imprint of Greenwood Publishing Group, Inc.

Printed in the United States of America

∞

The paper used in this book complies with the
Permanent Paper Standard issued by the National
Information Standards Organization (Z39.48–1984).

10 9 8 7 6 5 4 3 2 1

For my parents and parents-in-law

Contents

Preface

When I began teaching psychology sixteen years ago, by an odd coincidence my first-year students did the same kinds of things I had done as an undergraduate: They listened to lectures, read a textbook, and took multiple-choice tests. In upper-year courses, my students wrote single-draft term papers, duly graded and returned. Again there was an uncanny resemblance to my own experience.

My teaching life probably would have gone on like this for some time, but in 1979 my university—a small, undergraduate, liberal arts institution—adopted the requirement that all first-year students take a writing course. What was unusual about Effective Writing was that it was staffed not by members of the English department but by faculty recruited from various disciplines. My teaching and research interests at the time were in cognitive psychology, language, and reading, and I volunteered to teach in the program during its third year.

The experience was . . . interesting. As I recall, there were eight or ten instructors, each with about thirty students. James Reither, the director of the program, explained that the basis of the course was to be writing "as a process," and to this end we used Linda Flower's (1981) recently published textbook, *Problem-solving Strategies for Writing*. We also had the students practice sentence combining, using exercises from *The Writer's Options* (Daiker, Kerek, & Morenberg, 1979). But the main event was a research paper that students wrote on a topic of their choice. Because we were committed to process, the students wrote at least two drafts. In one-to-one conferences we pointed out where organization, say, or mechanics could be improved. My students wrote on subjects like "chairs" and "canoeing."

Undoubtedly, other instructors were more successful than I was. As far as I could tell, however, my students seemed to have learned little from the experience. Certainly I wasn't the first teacher to have known what Reither once described as "the sour taste of failure"; but I didn't sign up to teach the course again, and indeed it died a few years later from lack of faculty and administrative support.

Something, however, had happened. Going back to teaching psychology full-time, I found that I thought differently about student writing. At first the biggest change was that when I asked for a term paper I was no longer content with a single-draft effort. I wanted to slow the process down, to intervene as I had intervened in the writing course. Therefore I began to schedule one-to-one conferences; later I arranged it so that critiques of drafts were made by the students' peers as well as by me. Gradually, I began to see evidence that students were learning the forms and processes of academic writing as we know it in psychology.

Even more radical changes were afoot. Three colleagues from the late writing program—Reither, Russell Hunt, and Thom Parkhill—began teaching their courses in English and religious studies differently, making writing the central feature. These courses were organized as "collaborative investigations" in which students, often working in small groups, took responsibility for learning and writing about a given problem or area of inquiry. Eventually I began organizing my psychology courses along the same lines; soon after, in March 1988, the four of us gave a panel presentation on using writing in content and other courses at the Conference on College Composition and Communication (CCCC) in St. Louis.

It was in St. Louis that I encountered "composition studies" for the first time. At CCCC I heard composition specialists talking about writing, learning, and teaching in ways that seemed intellectually challenging and useful. *Discourse communities*, *collaborative learning*, *writing across the curriculum*—to me these were new terms, but they all seemed intensely relevant to what I was trying to do in my psychology courses back home.

To learn more about the ideas engaging CCCC members, I began reading in the rhetoric and composition literature. I was beginning to feel more comfortable with the different languages and modes of thought in composition, especially as I continued to participate in their conference and journal programs. At the same time, however, I was teaching a full complement of psychology courses; I was (and am) still a full-fledged member of the psychology department. More and more I seemed to be living a double life, working simultaneously in psychology and composition. Inevitably, I began to wonder about the connection between my two interests. What, if anything, did psychology and composition have to say to each other?

It wasn't long before I learned that composition specialists have drawn rather heavily on psychology, whereas psychologists have used composition hardly at all. In fact, considering that most of our scholarly activity is in written form, it is surprising how little direct attention psychology has given to writing. Our understanding of writing is still mostly tacit. Because composition studies is the field that specializes in the study and teaching of writing, it made sense to me that composition might provide psychology with a deeper and more explicit understanding of writing than we would otherwise enjoy.

This book is the result of putting *psychology* and *writing* together. Intended for psychologists, its purpose is to understand the writing and teaching practices of psychology by drawing on the scholarly field of composition studies.

My method is to compare two sets of documents about writing. The psychology documents are officially sanctioned guides, such as the *Publication Manual of the American Psychological Association*, as well as handbooks intended for students and others; the composition documents are journal articles and books from the scholarly literature. When these two sets of texts confront each other, it becomes clear that psychology could learn much from composition. We could learn, for instance, about audience, genre, and style—the topics discussed in Chapters 2, 3, and 4, respectively.

Because most of the book concerns what psychology could learn from composition, in the first chapter I review the situation that has prevailed until now, namely, what composition has learned from psychology. Over the years composition specialists have appropriated concepts, theories, and methods from psychology. For example, the work of Bruner, Piaget, and Vygotsky has been used to help understand cognitive and social processes in writing.

Chapter 2 compares ideas of "audience" put forward in psychology and composition. Whereas psychologists are consistently advised to analyze and then address their audiences, recent work in composition suggests that audience is a metaphor, and a limiting one because it implies that the writer–reader relationship is a performance rather than an interaction. As indicated by studies of writing in nonacademic settings, it is real readers— not "audiences"—who read. I suggest that the metaphor of *dialogue* or *conversation* expresses more powerfully than *audience* what happens when texts are written, read, and used in psychology and other academic discourse communities.

Chapter 3 considers genres of writing. Although writing in psychology is diverse, officially there is a hierarchy of genres, with empirical reports valued more highly than all other kinds. I review the feminist argument that there is an association between genres and genders, and that "official academic discourse" reflects masculinist assumptions and an ethic of competition. The chapter concludes with a consideration of other, nonacademic types of writing that may avoid some of the limitations of conventional academic and scientific discourse.

In Chapter 4, stylistic conventions of psychology are discussed. The APA *Manual* prescribes a scientific or plain style of writing that features clarity, literal (nonliterary) writing, and brevity; work in composition shows that these concepts are more problematic than they first appear. Clarity is a virtue but is not a simple property of texts; the demand for literal writing ignores scientists' unavoidable use of metaphors and other figurative language to create new meanings; the ideal of brevity must be balanced against the equally necessary art of amplification.

In Chapter 5 some implications of this analysis are drawn, with emphasis on teaching. Because writing permeates psychology, teachers of psychology must also, I argue, be teachers of writing. The writing-across-the-curriculum (WAC) movement has already had an effect on how writing is conceived in psychology education. I elaborate the proposals of WAC specialists by suggesting ways—under the headings of audience, genre, and style—that instructors can make writing a more vital part of students' academic lives.

To avoid misunderstanding, I should say that my purpose is not to suggest how psychologists might write better, but rather to suggest how we might *think differently* about writing. Even so, this book is not intended as a comprehensive, balanced survey of composition studies. My use of composition is selective: I draw heavily on theoretical work, for instance, but relatively little on experimental or other empirical work. Finally, although the book is about psychology and writing, it is not intended as a contribution to the psychology *of* writing.

Acknowledgments

I'm fortunate to have good friends in both writing and psychology; many of them have helped me with this book. For their generous and exceptionally useful comments on earlier drafts, I thank Charles Bazerman, Caroline Burnley, Ann Cameron, Gary Hughes, Russ Hunt, Ely Kozminsky, Anthony Paré, Thom Parkhill, Jim Reither, Graham Smart, and Claudia Whalen. In particular, I'd like to acknowledge the support of my colleagues Thom Parkhill, Jim Reither, and Russ Hunt; the latter two also deserve credit (or possibly blame) for introducing me to composition studies and continuing to guide me through it.

I am grateful to the librarians at the Harriet Irving Library and the Education Resource Centre for helping me track down material; thanks also to the administration of St. Thomas University, Fredericton, New Brunswick, Canada, for the time to work with this material by granting sabbatical leave in 1990–1991. I was made to feel welcome in composition circles by the people of the Conference on College Composition and Communication and, at Inkshed conferences, by the people of the Canadian Association for the Study of Writing and Reading; without them this book wouldn't have happened. I was also welcomed by the Centre for the Study and Teaching of Writing at McGill University in Montreal, and by Section 25 of the Canadian Psychological Association. Both organizations gave me a chance to present earlier versions of this project.

I'm grateful to my editors at Praeger—Karen Davis, Paul Macirowski, and Pat Merrill—for their encouragement and for their careful attention to all the details.

Finally, I'd like to thank my students for their resilience and my family, Jane, Nick, and Sam, for reminding me that there are more important things even than writing and psychology.

WRITING AND PSYCHOLOGY

Chapter One

Reversing the Polarity between Writing and Psychology

The field of composition studies is prospering.
—Charles Moran (1991, p. 182)

Psychology is steeped in writing. Consider first the quantity of published work: Nearly 3,000 books per year are sent to *Contemporary Psychology*, which reviews sixty percent of them (Harvey, 1992, 1993); the American Psychological Association (APA) alone publishes 1,500 journal articles per year, amounting to some 16,000 pages ("Buzzwords," 1992); and more than 35,000 items per year are listed in *Psychological Abstracts*—which works out to one item every fifteen minutes (Thorngate, 1990).

Consider, too, the unpublished, ephemeral kinds of writing in which psychology is also immersed: assessments of clients and programs, case studies, conference papers and posters, e-mail, grant proposals, journal and grant referee reports, lab notes, lectures and lecture notes, letters of recommendation, memos, progress reports, and so on.

It's clear, then, that writing in all its forms permeates psychology. In fact without this "visually transmitted symbolic activity" (Bazerman, 1988, p. 23), our discipline would be unimaginable. Given the centrality of writing, it seems reasonable to suggest that psychology could benefit by understanding it more thoroughly. We could profit by understanding what motivates writing, what purposes it serves, and what helps students learn to be writers of psychology. In short, psychology as a discipline could benefit from a knowledge base about writing.

The closest thing to such a knowledge base now is found in student handbooks, guides, research design textbooks, and in such authoritative documents as the *Publication Manual of the American Psychological Association* (American Psychological Association, 1983); they all present writing largely as a skill or technique. From this technical perspective, the main purpose of writing is to communicate research findings. The handbooks therefore identify good writing as that which conveys ideas clearly and efficiently. Conventional forms of writing (for example, the empirical report form) are especially recommended.

The handbooks give explicit guidelines on how to write like a psychologist. By presenting a consistent model of writing, they help both writers and readers process psychological discourse more efficiently. The handbooks are less helpful, however, in explaining *why* we write. They are largely atheoretical: They tend not to discuss what writing is for, where it comes from, or how forms of written communication can limit as well as convey knowledge. Handbooks help develop psychologists' writing skills but do little to develop our *understanding* of writing.

If handbooks don't help us understand writing, where can we look? I propose that we turn for theoretical guidance to a modern field of scholarly and practical knowledge about writing and its teaching. Although its roots are in a rhetorical tradition that goes back 2,500 years, this field is now widely known as *composition studies* (Lindemann & Tate, 1991).

In contrast to the technical perspective found in psychology handbooks, the general view in composition studies is that writing is a way of knowing and acting. Seen as a way of knowing, the purpose of writing is not simply to convey but to discover and validate knowledge (Gage, 1984); from this perspective, the forms of written language influence not only how we say, but also what we say and therefore what we know. Seen as a form of social action, writing is not just a means of transmitting information, but also a means of establishing and altering relationships with others; significantly, writing is seen to take place within *communities* of discourse.

The perspectives of psychology handbooks and composition studies are thus generally different. While this is not to say that one is correct and the other is in error, the difficulty is that psychology as a discipline has developed one conception of writing but not the other. Psychology's current knowledge base about writing, reflected in its guides and manuals, is heavily weighted toward the technical perspective. As a result, we're missing something. There is more to writing than what the handbooks are telling us.

The purpose of this book is to draw on modern composition theory to develop a richer understanding of writing and its teaching. Psychology and psychologists, I suggest, could benefit in at least three ways from a knowledge base developed according to the perspectives of composition studies.

First, new ways of understanding writing could contribute to the self-understanding of the discipline. Because writing is such a large part of what psychologists do—it's the ocean in which we all swim—understanding writing more fully would mean that we understand ourselves more fully.

Second, a more practical benefit of a new knowledge base is that by understanding our writing practices better we could control them better. Understanding is our best defense against practices that are unreflective and therefore possibly limiting. Greater awareness of our options could give us access to new forms and styles of writing. On the assumption that writing is not just a skill but a way of knowing, greater awareness of options could open a space for different ways of writing and, thereby, different ways of knowing.

Third, having a more adequate understanding of writing could help us bring students more fully into the discourse communities of psychology. Students learn to be psychologists, in large part, by learning to read and write like psychologists. Therefore we need to do more than train students in the fine points of APA style. Because psychology is steeped in "visually transmitted symbolic activity," teachers of psychology are, or should be, teachers of writing as well. We have at least some choice, though, in what kinds of writing we teach, and how.

If, as I have suggested, a new understanding of writing is available in modern composition theory, let us inquire more deeply into the scholarly field that makes writing its specialty.

COMPOSITION STUDIES

For our purposes, composition studies may be defined as the scholarly and practical field that specializes in the study and teaching of writing.[1]

Unlike psychology, composition studies is not a high-profile discipline. (There is no popular magazine called *Composition Today*.) Composition is an unusual academic field because it is closely associated, both historically and in the present, with a single course in the college curriculum, variously called "required English," "freshman English," and "freshman composition" (Bartholomae, 1989). Indeed, most composition specialists are teachers. Pedagogy is of such deep concern to the field that it is common, even in theoretical articles, to find a discussion of implications for classroom practice—the "Monday morning" question. In other words, composition specialists like to be "close to the place where, as those in the automobile culture would say, the rubber meets the road" (Moran, 1991, p. 160). In this respect, perhaps, they are similar to psychologists, who also tend to be concerned with improving—not just understanding—human behavior.

In American colleges and universities, composition is usually a required course—often the only one. Therefore the numbers of students and teachers are large, perhaps as many as five million students and 25,000 teachers in any given year (S. Miller, 1991).[2]

Despite these numbers, it would be a mistake to think of composition as merely a "service" department or a field of practice (Schuster, 1991). Composition studies is deeply concerned with pedagogy, but it is also, increasingly, a flourishing field of scholarship and research. Social, cultural, cognitive, philosophical, linguistic, and historical aspects of writing are all within its scope. Pluralism also characterizes its modes of inquiry. In *The Making of Knowledge in Composition: Portrait of an Emerging Field*, Stephen North (1987) identifies eight main types of inquiry in composition: practitioner, historical, philosophical, hermeneutic, experimental, clinical, formal, and ethnographic. Composition studies is becoming increasingly specialized (Berkenkotter, 1991) and is steadily acquiring books and book series, journals, graduate programs, endowed chairs, conferences, bibliographies—all the trappings of a full-fledged academic discipline.[3]

Composition wasn't always such a prospering field. If psychology is to take the modern field of composition studies seriously, we need to understand at least something about its background. Here I will focus on two moments in the evolution of composition studies: (1) the shift from rhetoric to composition in the late nineteenth century; and (2) the shift from composition to composition studies in the mid twentieth century.

From Rhetoric to Composition

The study and practice of *rhetoric*, in the sense of persuasive oratory, dominated formal education ever since the ancient Greeks. Even in nineteenth-century North America, oral performance and classical languages were emphasized. College students were required to participate in recitations, orations, debates, declamations, and public examinations (Russell, 1991, chap. 2). The students themselves were an elite group; primarily, they were men destined for careers as lawyers, politicians, and clergymen. The emphasis on persuasive oratory was well-suited to professions where speechmaking was, and still is, highly valued (Halloran, 1990).

The shift from oral rhetoric to written composition was prompted by changes in higher education and technology. The Morrill Act of 1862 created land-grant universities to serve not just the elite professions but agriculture, engineering, and business. Middle-class students began attending college in large numbers in order to acquire the knowledge needed to become credentialed members of these professions (Halloran, 1990). Instruction in proper English (not Latin) was seen as a way to ensure that these new students could take their place in the intellectual and economic life of society (Lunsford, 1991).[4] Furthermore, sheer numbers made oral recitations unworkable, whereas written exams were a convenient way for masses of students to demonstrate that they had acquired discipline-appropriate knowledge (Halloran, 1990).

Changes in technology assisted the move from rhetoric to writing in the colleges. Typewriters, inexpensive pencils, fountain pens, and cheap durable paper became widely available in the nineteenth century (Larsen, 1986; Lunsford, 1991). Reading and writing became more common activities, too, as books and periodicals became more numerous and postal service improved (Halloran, 1990).

Thus writing slowly replaced speechmaking in the colleges. But as it did, the perhaps inevitable complaints started to be made about the quality of student writing. Charles Eliot of Harvard responded to these criticisms in 1872 by appointing a journalist, Adams Sherman Hill, to begin college-level composition courses (Russell, 1991, p. 49). In 1885 Hill succeeded in moving the composition course from the sophomore to the first year; "freshman comp" has been an institution ever since (S. Miller, 1991, p. 63).[5]

From Composition to Composition Studies

For our purposes, a shift even more momentous than the one from rhetoric to composition occurred in the years following World War II, when the teaching of composition gradually gave way to a new academic field eventually known as "composition studies." Historians have identified several factors that led to its emergence (Connors, 1991). First of all, there was a change in the type of person who taught English. Before the war, English professors tended to be from the upper classes, trained in philology and historical criticism. After the war, GIs from all social classes rushed back to university; as they made their way through graduate school and then filtered into teaching positions in colleges, they democratized

English. For many, composition was not menial labor that had to be endured before getting to the "real" task of literature. Instead, they took composition teaching seriously, talked about it, studied it, and determined to do the best job possible (Connors, 1991).

At about the same time, the "communications movement" was sweeping the United States. Based on the principles of General Semantics, the communications movement sought to integrate speaking, writing, listening, and reading. By 1948 the communications course was taught in more than 200 colleges and universities. It was popular in part because it was seen as an effective way to deal with the special problems of the large number of veterans returning to school (Berlin, 1987, p. 96).

In the late 1940s a new organization was formed to serve writing teachers. At the 1948 meetings of the National Council of Teachers of English (NCTE), a session on the first-year composition course proved so lively that a special meeting was organized the following May on "composition and communication"; the dual title acknowledged the interest of both teachers of composition and teachers of communication (Berlin, 1987, p. 105). This May 1949 convention, attended by 500 people, was the first meeting of the Conference on College Composition and Communication (CCCC).[6] Later that year CCCC was formally incorporated as a division within NCTE with its own budget and journal, *College Composition and Communication.*

In the late 1940s and early 1950s, the new active generation of English professors, together with their colleagues in the communications movement, began to forge a new scholarly field (Connors, 1991). During the 1960s and 1970s, composition studies grew rapidly by conducting scholarship that recuperated its rhetorical tradition; it grew also by conducting research based on similarities with other disciplines, especially linguistics and psychology: "Like Whitman's spider, it threw out thread after thread to other disciplines, hoping that some would catch" (Connors, 1991, p. 55). Before considering the threads that composition threw in our direction, let us consider briefly the "rhetorical tradition" it was eager to recuperate and then see how this tradition has been used to illuminate modern psychology.

Rhetoric and Psychology

So far I have used "composition" to refer to written discourse and "rhetoric" to refer to oral discourse. But *composition* can refer variously to the act, theory, or teaching of composing, while the meanings of *rhetoric* are even more unruly (Gage, 1991). If originally rhetoric did mean persuasive oratory, its scope has expanded over the centuries. Now, oral, written, or, for that matter, any other form of symbolic communication can all be considered rhetoric (Bizzell & Herzberg, 1990, p. 2). Thus it is difficult to distinguish composition and rhetoric conceptually, but it is possible—and, for our purposes, more important—to distinguish them historically, on the basis of different scholarly traditions. As already noted, composition studies is a fairly recent phenomenon, emerging after World War II; the rhetorical tradition, on the other hand, is 2,500 years old.

It may be helpful to identify various phases of this rhetorical tradition, and within each phase, key contributors (Bizzell & Herzberg, 1990). Some of these are names we'll encounter later in this book: in the classical period, the Greek Sophists (fifth century B.C.) and Aristotle, as well as the Romans Cicero and Quintilian; in the medieval period, Augustine and Boethius; in the Renaissance, Erasmus, Peter Ramus, and Francis Bacon; in the eighteenth century, George Campbell and Hugh Blair; in the nineteenth century, Richard Whately, Alexander Bain, and Adams Sherman Hill; and in the twentieth century, I. A. Richards, Kenneth Burke, and Chaim Perelman, as well as Mikhail Bakhtin, Michel Foucault, and Jacques Derrida.

Rhetoricians and psychologists alike have drawn on the rhetorical tradition to help understand psychology. Scholars of rhetoric have investigated, for example, the Skinner/Chomsky controversy (Czubaroff, 1989), language in gorillas (Prelli, 1989, chap. 7), memory transfer in planarians (Prelli, 1989, chap. 8), and placebos in psychotherapy (Simons, 1989). Without doubt, however, the *psychologist* who has done most to illuminate modern psychology by means of the rhetorical tradition is Michael Billig.

Billig (1987, 1990, 1991) draws especially on the classical period of rhetoric. He argues that the ancient study of rhetoric is a forerunner of modern psychology; classical rhetoricians studied many topics social psychologists study today, and their analyses are not inferior. As Billig shows, however, the connection between rhetoric and psychology runs deeper than that. Modern social psychology is rhetorical in its very nature because it proceeds by argumentation, not by strict logic. When psychologists write papers, we are making arguments to counter the arguments of others. Therefore each paper needs to be understood rhetorically; that is, placed in its context of argumentation. Social psychology as a whole, Billig (1990) says, constitutes an argument against "common sense." Like common sense, however, social psychology produces contradictory arguments, which enable thought. Thinking itself is argumentative, hence rhetorical and social—a point sometimes overlooked by cognitive psychologists (Billig, 1987, pp. 96–99).

Although this brief summary doesn't do justice to Billig's work, it shows in a general way how the rhetorical tradition can illuminate modern psychology. This overview also helps to clarify the difference between previous studies and the present one. Whereas others have used rhetoric, I will use composition studies to help understand psychology. Therefore this project will, for the most part, be restricted to the composition studies tradition (if one can call a forty-five year history a "tradition"), and will not draw *directly* on the rhetorical tradition. Indirectly, however, rhetoric is never far away: To the extent that rhetoric is composition studies' "tap root" (Reither, 1991), whenever we draw on composition, we are drawing on rhetoric as well.

COMPOSITION'S USES OF PSYCHOLOGY

The bridges between composition and psychology are in place. To date, however, they have carried only one-way traffic, from psychology to composition. In the remainder of this chapter, I will survey some of the ways composition has used or "appropriated" psychology. Although not intended to be an exhaustive treatment, this will clear the way for the rest of the book: psychology's possible uses of composition.

I don't mean to suggest that psychology is the *only* discipline that composition studies has drawn upon. It has also thrown "spider threads" to linguistics, speech communication, anthropology, and, of course, to classical rhetoric. But without psychology, composition would now be very different from what it is. As the saying goes, composition didn't get where it is today by ignoring psychology.

To illustrate the connections between the two fields, a good person to start with is Alexander Bain (1818–1903). He had a foot in both camps. Psychologists remember Bain for his principles of association in mental phenomena; composition scholars remember him as a developer of paragraph theory and "current-traditional rhetoric."[7] What is pertinent for us, though, is that Bain used his psychology to explain his rhetoric, but not the other way around. For example, Bain's *English Composition and Rhetoric* (1866), like most nineteenth-century rhetoric texts, classified the figures of speech. What was unusual was that Bain gave the classification, in his words, "an entirely new turn," by describing it in terms of psychological principles of association (Mulderig, 1982, p. 96).

In more recent times, composition has borrowed both concepts and methods from psychology. In what follows, therefore, I will focus on, first, conceptual appropriations in "process theory" (ca. 1960–1975) and, second, methodological appropriations in composition research (ca. 1965–

1980). The word *appropriation*, incidentally, isn't meant to suggest that composition had sinister intentions. Young disciplines always try to borrow from better established ones. Psychologists, of all people, understand this very well, because psychology itself appropriated from sensory physiology and other fields when it emerged as a discipline in the late nineteenth century (Danziger, 1990a, chap. 2).

Conceptual Appropriations: Process Theory

The "current-traditional" rhetoric that Bain helped develop continued as a major force in the teaching of writing for a century or more. Emphasis was placed on the written product rather than on composing processes. Writing was presented in terms of proper usage, mechanical correctness, and a limited number of forms: exposition, description, narration, and argument (R. Young, 1978). A staple of current-traditional instruction was the "five-paragraph theme."

By about the 1960s, however, the consensus had begun to change. Now composition specialists believed they must study and teach the processes of writing rather than the written products—hence the slogan, "process not product." Process theory was important for the self-definition of composition studies because it helped stabilize what was until then a loosely connected set of practices (S. Miller, 1991, p. 115). Some authors even see the change from product to process as a paradigm shift in the Kuhnian sense (Hairston, 1982; R. Young, 1978). Others, taking a more moderate line, argue that the change was more gradual and that, in any case, current-traditional rhetoric was far from a monolithic force during the first six decades of this century (Varnum, 1992).

We can safely leave historians of composition to debate this among themselves, I think. The important point for our purposes is that psychology played a key role in composition's turn to process in the 1960s. As writing theorists, researchers, and teachers directed attention to the cognitive processes involved in various phases of writing—prewriting, drafting, revising—and to the different levels of social and cognitive development that students bring to writing tasks, they turned to the work of cognitive and developmental psychologists.

This is not to say, however, that compositionists suddenly started reading Piaget and Vygotsky. Instead, they discovered psychology indirectly, largely through the mediating influence of educational theory. Jerome Bruner's contribution as a mediator was particularly important. In works such as *The Process of Education* (1960), "The Act of Discovery," and "The Conditions of Creativity" (both in *On Knowing*, 1962), Bruner helped introduce cognitive and Piagetian psychology to American education, and hence to composition (Berlin, 1987, p. 122).[8]

Although "process" may be the single most important idea in composition during the past thirty years, composition scholars understand process in different ways. These may be conveniently identified as *expressive*, *cognitive*, and *social* views (Faigley, 1986). In developing each of these perspectives, composition appropriated different aspects of psychology, as we will now see.

Influences of psychology on expressive views of process. Expressive views of process refer to the Romantic idea that good writing reflects integrity, spontaneity, and originality (Faigley, 1986, p. 529)—the same qualities that have been attributed by humanistic psychologists to "the fully-functioning person." Psychology's influence on expressive views of process can be seen in the frequency with which writing is compared to self-growth and writing teachers are compared to therapists (see Brand, 1980).

For example, D. Gordon Rohman (1965), referring indirectly to Carl Rogers, Abraham Maslow, and Rollo May, calls upon writing teachers to take advantage of people's desire for self-actualization. Rohman suggests that self-actualization makes writing possible just as it makes therapy possible. Similarly, James Moffett (1982) argues that both writing and therapy require maximum availability of information from all internal and external sources; both require maximum synthesizing of this information into a "full, harmonious expression of individual experience" (p. 234). Good writing and good therapy both aim at clear thinking, effective relating, and satisfying self-expression, but this does not mean that the writing teacher should try to play therapist. Thanks to the essential similarity between the two processes, there is no need: "Precisely because it is not thought of as therapy and works toward another goal," Moffett says, "writing can effect fine therapy sometimes" (p. 234).[9]

Influences of psychology on cognitive views of process. The individual person is the focus for cognitive theorists, just as for expressive theorists. From a cognitive perspective, however, writing is seen not in terms of self-growth, but in terms of the individual's mental structures and representations. Two cognitive strands may be identified: (1) cognitive development; and (2) cognitive science.

Piaget's notions of egocentric and decentered (sociocentric) speech have been especially fertile in composition studies because they can be related to rhetoric's traditional concern with audience. Writing teachers want their students to be aware of audience—in Piagetian terms, to decenter. Thus, Barry Kroll (1978) argues that composition needs a cognitive-developmental theory that will specify what writers do when they are aware of audience and how this awareness develops. Sondra Perl (1979) found that unskilled college writers seemed not to be concerned with their readers' understanding, but instead wrote "from an egocentric point of view" (p. 332). And Andrea Lunsford (1980) used Piagetian concepts to account for the content of less skilled, or "basic," writers' essays. Asked to write about "my most memorable character," basic writers often wrote about themselves instead. Lunsford attributes this to the writers' inability to decenter, to achieve a nonegocentric rhetorical stance (p. 281).

Turning to the cognitive science strand, one of the earliest uses of psychology by composition was that of Richard Larson (1968), who noted a similarity between what composition calls "invention" and what psychology calls "creativity" (p. 127). Janice Lauer (1970) was even more explicit in calling on writing theorists and teachers to "break out of the ghetto" by using psychology as a source of good ideas about invention (p. 396). Psychological work on creative problem solving is useful both to writing teachers, dealing with the process of composition, and to rhetoricians, developing new theories of invention.

But by far the most influential cognitive science approach to writing is that of Linda Flower and John R. Hayes. In their early work, Flower and Hayes (1977) considered writing as a form of problem solving. Their cognitive model of writing features three components: task environment, long-term memory, and writing processes, the latter made up of planning, translating, and reviewing subcomponents (Hayes & Flower, 1980). It is no accident that the Hayes-Flower model of writing strongly resembles Allen Newell and Herbert Simon's (1972) "general problem solver": The overall structure of the writing model was, in Hayes's (1992) words, "borrowed quite directly from Newell and Simon," their colleagues at Carnegie Mellon (p. 128).

Influences of psychology on social views of process. In general, psychologists seem to have had less influence on social than on cognitive views of process, but a striking exception is the work of Vygotsky. Composition theorists who take a social perspective assume that human language needs to be understood not from the standpoint of the individual's mental structures, but in terms of society and culture. More precisely, in the social view the focus is on "how the individual is a constituent of a culture" (Faigley, 1986, p. 535). These composition specialists have found in Vygotsky a strong ally, because he insisted that language be understood as a cultural and historical process.

Thus, for example, Kenneth Bruffee (1983) uses Vygotsky to support his view that writing and reading are social or collaborative acts. For

Vygotsky, the origins of thought are in social interaction; thought is internalized speech. But, Bruffee (1984) reasons, if thought is internalized speech or conversation, *writing* can be understood as "internalized conversation re-externalized" (p. 641). Another conclusion Bruffee draws from Vygotsky's work is that even the most solitary-seeming writing is profoundly collaborative. "We work together," Bruffee (1983) says, "whether we work together or apart" (p. 162).

Similarly, Patricia Bizzell (1982) uses Vygotsky in her critique of cognitive or "inner-directed" theories of writing. According to Bizzell, such theories tend to separate thought and language, regarding writing as a matter of putting thoughts into words. For Vygotsky, on the other hand, thought and language are separate only for the very young child; they come together in the development of "verbal thought." From a Vygotskian perspective, thought and language are dialectically related; verbal thought is determined by a historical and cultural process. Bizzell draws the conclusion that writing and writing instruction, too, need to be seen as fundamentally social and cultural—not cognitive—processes. Writing needs to be seen, that is, in terms of the conventions and expectations that writers share by virtue of belonging to *discourse communities* (Bizzell, 1982, p. 218).

Methodological Appropriations

Process theory—whether expressive, cognitive, or social—isn't the only area in which composition has appropriated concepts from psychology. Writing theorists and researchers have borrowed ideas from psychological thinkers as diverse as Freud, Carol Gilligan, and B. F. Skinner (see Table 1). Rather than detailing each of these, however, I'd like to turn to a topic that may be even more important than conceptual appropriation, namely, methodological appropriation.

As process theory grew more popular in the 1960s, composition studies took a decidedly scientific turn. Many commentators believe this was due, in large part, to the "Braddock Report" (Braddock, Lloyd-Jones, & Schoer, 1963). Richard Braddock's committee was asked by the NCTE to prepare a "scientifically based report" on what was known about composition (p. 1). At that time the typical research project was a large-scale study featuring a pre/post design with method of teaching as the treatment variable. Braddock and his colleagues were extremely critical of most of this research because it "has not frequently been conducted with the knowledge and care that one associates with the physical sciences" (p. 5).

Table 1
More Examples of Composition's Uses of Psychology

Psychologist	Psychological Concept	Use in Composition Studies	Sample Compositionist
Belenky et al.	women's ways of knowing	narratives of women vs. men	Flynn (1988)
Freud	transference, resistance	student-teacher relationship in writing class	Murphy (1989)
Gilligan	moral development in women	women writers' difficulties with "audience"	Cayton (1990)
Izard	primary emotions	positive and negative emotions in writing	Brand (1989)
Jung	personality theory	personality differences in writers	Jensen & DiTiberio (1989)
Kohlberg	stages of cognitive-moral development	stages of basic vs. skilled writers	Lunsford (1980)
Lacan	transference	nondirective response in teaching writing	Brooke (1987a)
Lazarus & Averill	anxiety	coping behaviors of writing-anxious students	Selfe (1985)
Mandler	theory of emotion	interactions of physiology and cognition in writing	McLeod (1987)
Perry	stages of intellectual and ethical development	stages enable different writing tasks	Tedesco (1991)
Rogers	facilitation of communication	"Rogerian" argument in writing	Young, Becker, & Pike (1970)
Skinner	operant conditioning	writing shaped by environment	Zoellner (1969)
Weiner	attribution theory	writers' attributions for success and failure	Daly (1985)

Today's research in composition, taken as a whole, may be compared to chemical research as it emerged from the period of alchemy: some terms are being defined usefully, a number of procedures are being refined, but the field as a whole is laced with dreams, prejudices, and makeshift operations. (Braddock, Lloyd-Jones, & Schoer, 1963, p. 5)

Braddock and his associates were able, however, to find five superior studies—ones that had sufficient N, used appropriate statistics, and controlled most or all of the relevant variables. These they described in considerable detail.

The message of the Braddock Report was not lost on the composition community, and by the 1970s the field seemed eager to be seen as scientifically respectable. Researchers deferred to experimental and educational psychology for advice on research designs, control of variables, quantification, statistical inference, and meta-analysis. Janet Emig (1971) contributed to the discipline's "science consciousness" (Voss, 1983)—"psychology consciousness" may be the more accurate term—by using a case study method of inquiry that derived from, among others, Freud, Bruno Bettelheim, and Piaget. Flower and Hayes raised science consciousness a notch higher when they imported think-aloud procedures and protocol analysis from cognitive psychology to composition research. The journal *Research in the Teaching of English*, founded in 1967 with Braddock as editor, quickly became the chief forum for empirical research on writing; its history since then has been one of "ever-increasing methodological rigor" (Connors, 1984, p. 355). This empirical tradition was so robust that George Hillocks (1986) was able to find some 2,000 pieces of research published between 1963 and 1982—and this was excluding work of an "anecdotal, hortatory, historical, curricular, or literary" nature (p. xviii).

During this period many composition specialists came to appreciate the strengths and weaknesses of psychology's methods. In his autobiographical *Lives on the Boundary*, Mike Rose (1990) says that, during a one-year exposure to experimental psychology, he learned to respect scientists' methodical approach to questions. At the same time, however, "as with so many reductive pursuits, the academic psychology I studied taught me a great deal by what it could not do" (p. 80).

As suggested, perhaps, by the reference to "reductive pursuits," composition's scientific turn was not welcomed by everyone (Arrington, 1991). While agreeing that there must be room in composition studies for experimentation and quantitative analysis, Robert Connors (1983a) argues that composition is not a science in the traditional sense and should stop pretending that it is. Less conciliatory are the positions of Ann Berthoff and William Irmscher. According to Berthoff (1971), when compositionists such as Lauer take seriously the work of psychologists, "the results are philosophically disastrous and politically dangerous" (p. 240). Similarly, Irmscher (1987) insists that composition must find a "comfortable identity" of its own: "Up to this time, we have essentially imitated other disciplines, borrowed without fully considering the context and bounds of our own discipline. We have tried on garments that are ill-fitting" (p. 84).

The empiricism imported from psychology, Irmscher implies, is the worst-fitting garment of all—one that composition would do well to cast off. "To Braddock, Hillocks, and the tradition they represent," Irmscher writes, "much of the research on composition lacks rigorous procedure. To others, not exclusively our literature compatriots, it lacks rigorous thought" (p. 83). Irmscher seems to be saying that it is no longer a matter of composition's appropriating psychology, but of its being appropriated by psychology. Borrowing ideas from another discipline is one thing; being taken over, methodologically speaking, is quite another.[10]

In spite of these criticisms, it can't be denied that composition studies has been strongly influenced by psychology. Many composition specialists continue to look to our discipline for guidance (see Table 1). It remains to explain why.

A possible reason is that composition studies wanted "to share in the cachet of science" (Connors, 1983a, p. 19). Composition teaching has always been seen as a "low," stigmatized activity (S. Miller, 1991). In an effort, perhaps, to boost its relatively low status and to differentiate itself from English studies and speech communication, composition associated itself with the relatively high-status discipline of scientific psychology. Was "social climbing" a motive behind the switch to APA style, in 1973, by *Research in the Teaching of English*?[11] If so, composition wouldn't be the first field to form an alliance with a more established, "scientific" discipline: As noted earlier, psychology itself used this strategy a century ago.

Moreover, because composition specialists often had to justify new writing programs to administrators, they were forced to adopt the empirical, quantified language that administrators understand. According to this explanation, the turn to scientific methods was at least partly a matter of survival (Bridwell-Bowles, 1991).

Even granted all this, however, we should not overlook what composition genuinely had to gain from psychology. When theory and research in composition turned from a current-traditional concern with product to an emphasis on process, psychology provided much of the necessary language, theory, and methodology. As composition specialists began to take more seriously the writing processes of all students, including basic writers (Shaughnessy, 1977), it became clear that writing could not be separated from other aspects of mind and behavior. If composition studies appropriated concepts and methods from psychology it was ultimately because it *needed* psychology in order to understand how writing might fit within the larger pictures of cognition, personality, socialization, and development (Lunsford, 1980, p. 284).

in composition studies, and then discuss how it is portrayed in handbooks intended for writers of psychology. My main concern, however, will be to explore some limitations of "audience"; in particular, its implication that writing is performance. Basing the argument on recent work in composition, I will suggest why "audience" could be usefully replaced (or supplemented) by a view of writing as a form of dialogue or conversation.

THE CONCEPT OF AUDIENCE IN COMPOSITION STUDIES

Audience usually refers to the people one writes to or addresses. Therefore, Lisa Ede and Andrea Lunsford (1984) define an *addressed audience* as "those actual or real-life people who read a discourse" (p. 156n). Addressed audiences tend to be monolithic and homogeneous: One writes for "experimental psychologists," "developmental psychologists," "undergraduates," or "the general reader." As Ede and Lunsford point out, those who take an addressed view assume that knowledge of the audience's attitudes, beliefs, and expectations is both possible and necessary. Writers are often encouraged to conduct an *audience analysis* in order to know more precisely the characteristics of those addressed.[2]

The audience-addressed approach has an honorable place in the history of rhetoric. Its roots are in oratory, where "audience" meant simply and literally "hearers," the people one is speaking to. It was suggested, however, that orators spoke to different kinds of people and that speeches should be adjusted accordingly. Plato says in the *Phaedrus* that the good rhetorician will "classify the types of discourse and the types of souls, and the various ways in which souls are affected . . . suggesting the type of speech appropriate to each type of soul" (quoted by Kroll, 1984, p. 173). Similarly, Aristotle, in Book II of the *Rhetoric*, describes different types of people that rhetors could adapt their speeches to: "[The elderly] are positive about nothing; in all things they err by an extreme moderation. . . . The rich are insolent and superior. . . . Now the hearer is always receptive when a speech is adapted to his own character and reflects it" (quoted by Park, 1986, p. 480).

The Aristotelian method—matching type of discourse to type of audience—has been by far the most influential throughout the history of rhetoric, up to and including modern composition studies. For example, in "A Heuristic Model for Creating a Writer's Audience," Fred Pfister and Joanne Petrick (1980) recommend that student writers conduct an audience analysis—a series of questions designed to elicit a more plausible and detailed picture of what otherwise is "unseen, a phantom" (p. 213).

Pfister and Petrick have students conduct the audience analysis according to four groups of questions. First, the audience is identified (age, education, class, occupation, values, and so on). Second, audience/subject questions are asked: What does the audience know about this subject? What is its opinion? Third, audience/writer questions require the student to ask, What is my purpose in writing for this particular audience? Fourth, audience/form questions: Given my purpose, what is the best way to achieve it with this audience? Students are encouraged to answer these questions before writing, because "successful written communication . . . depends a great deal on the writer's knowledge of his or her audience" (p. 218).

ADDRESSED AUDIENCES IN PSYCHOLOGY

The audience-addressed approach may well sound familiar to psychologists; it is the dominant perspective in our discipline, too. Handbooks and guides intended for writers of psychology take a firmly audience-addressed approach. They advise psychologists to analyze and write for an audience conceived as a monolithic, unitary entity.

For example, in *The Psychologist's Companion: A Guide to Scientific Writing for Students and Researchers*, Robert Sternberg (1988) recommends that you "write for your reader." This entails taking into account the extent of the reader's technical vocabulary, maintaining an appropriate level of formality, including only appropriate details, and avoiding abbreviations (p. 59). The advice is based on the assumption that audiences are unitary: One type of person reads *Psychological Review*, another reads *Psychology Today*, and so on. Sternberg also makes the audience-addressed assumption that an audience's knowledge can be assessed or at least estimated before writing. How else are writers to know the extent of their readers' technical vocabulary or to decide which details are appropriate?

The issue of appropriateness also concerned Daryl Bem (1987). In "Writing the Empirical Journal Article," Bem advises psychology writers not to assume too much. He recommends that we write for the general, educated reader, not just for the specialist. Intelligent nonpsychologists with no training in statistics or design should be able to grasp the broad outlines of what you did and why, especially in the introduction and discussion sections (p. 174). "Direct your writing," Bem advises, not to other specialists but "to the student in Psychology 100, your colleague in the Art History Department, and your grandmother" (p. 174). Even the more technical sections of the paper, "method" and "results," should be aimed at a reader one level of expertise less specialized than the audience for which the journal is primarily published. Assume that the reader of your article in *Psychometrika* knows about regression, but needs some introduction to LISREL. Assume that the reader of the *Journal of Personality and Social Psychology* knows about person perception but needs some introduction to dispositional and situational attributions. (Bem, 1987, pp. 174–175)

Bem's advice is sound, and I have no quarrel with it. I do, however, wish to draw attention to his metaphors—writing is *directed to* or *aimed at* a reader—which presuppose the audience-addressed perspective. From here it's not a large step to a view of writing as a kind of manipulation—a matter of throwing "persuasive darts" at "target" audiences (Kroll, 1984, p. 175).

In addition to writers who are preparing empirical reports for publication, the concept of audience is considered necessary for psychology students who write papers as part of their course work. Margot Northey and Brian Timney (1986) advise student-writers to "think about the reader" (p. 3). If it is not known who the reader is, however, students should imagine a rational general reader—"someone intelligent, well-informed and interested, skeptical enough to question your ideas but flexible enough to accept them if your evidence is convincing" (p. 4).

A more detailed treatment is offered by Lynne Bond and Anthony Magistrale (1987). In *Writer's Guide: Psychology*, Bond and Magistrale tell students that audience is the third decision they need to make (after subject and purpose but before voice). If writing a paper on, say, physical attractiveness, it makes or should make a difference if the audience is high school students, introductory psychology students, advanced social psychology students, or fashion designers. Because different audiences have different requirements, "you can write much more effectively if you can precisely define your audience" (p. 9). Bond and Magistrale themselves define five potential audiences for students doing course assignments: the instructor, the entire class (other students and instructor), the writer herself, a specific readership (for example, parents, families of psychiatric patients, politicians), and scholars in the field. To define an audience, Bond and Magistrale recommend that students conduct a detailed audience analysis, similar to that of Pfister and Petrick. A writer should be asking these kinds of questions: What does the audience already know about the subject? What are its expectations likely to be? What is the age, job, and income of the audience? What is its educational level?

CRITICISMS OF THE AUDIENCE-ADDRESSED APPROACH

Although the audience-addressed approach has been dominant in rhetoric and composition, a number of objections have been raised. In the first place, it is suggested that much of the talk about actual or real-life readers is essentially lip service. More often, these readers are merely representations that exist only in the mind of the writer. Writers are advised to "consider" their readers—but not, for instance, to *talk* to them—so it is possible that the audience exists only, as it were, as a figment of the writer's imagination. For one critic, Marilyn Cooper (1986), this "cognitivizing" of audience is a natural but unwelcome outcome of cognitive process theory (see Chapter 1), which "forces us to conceive all significant aspects of writing in terms of mental entities" (p. 371).

As Cooper rightly points out, audience is a mental construct even for strong advocates of audience analysis like Pfister and Petrick (1980). For them, audience is "unseen, a phantom"; writers must "fictionalize" their audience, "construct [it] in the imagination" (pp. 213–214). Similarly, in psychology, student writers are often advised to "think about the reader" (Northey & Timney, 1986, p. 3). The operative word is *think*.

By means of audience analysis, writers are asked to think about the age, occupation, income, and education of their potential readers. But critics point out that such demographic characteristics have little obvious connection to writing. Even if it were possible to accumulate demographic facts about one's readers (and often it isn't), the problem, as Douglas Park (1986) observes, is that such accumulation "has no clear goal or limit. . . . [T]he writer [has] no clear way to determine the relevance or weight of any of this information to the task at hand" (p. 481).

Furthermore, by asking about *the* age or *the* job, audience analysis seems to assume that audiences are uniform, monolithic. Isn't it more likely that different members of the audience will have different ages, different jobs, different interests and abilities? Even when an audience is as seemingly uniform as "social psychologists," "clinical psychologists," or "students in an introductory class," it's a serious oversimplification to assume that all members are alike.

That brings us to the final criticism of the audience-addressed approach, namely, that it is often in effect a type of stereotyping. We see this in a blatant form in Aristotle ("the rich are insolent and superior"), but it's present in more subtle form in handbooks that advise us to write for a particular group of readers who share some physical or occupational attribute. As Russell Long (1980) notes, the assumption is highly questionable that an occupation—for example, "social psychologist"—is an accurate indicator of attitudes or perceptions. Just as questionable is the assumption that people who share some superficial attribute are alike in all other respects. Long is speaking as a teacher of writing, but I think psychologists would agree that "we would not tolerate this sort of noxious stereotyping in any other context" (p. 223).

AUDIENCE AS METAPHOR

So far we have considered the concept of audience in writing and psychology, and have seen that the dominant approach in both fields—the idea of audience as an addressed entity—has raised a number of objections. Serious as these criticisms are, however, an even more fundamental issue is the *metaphoric* nature of audience. After considering some of the implications of the audience metaphor, I will discuss an alternative one in a later section.

As mentioned earlier, the roots of the audience-addressed approach are in oratory. In the context of oral communication, "audience" is an accurate term because it refers literally to "hearers"—"all those folks out there in chairs" who listen to a formal speech (Park, 1982, p. 249). When the spoken word gave way to the written word, however, the term *audience* stuck. Consequently, when applied to writing, "audience" is actually a metaphor. It's a rich and evocative metaphor, to be sure, and no doubt it will continue to be used in composition, psychology, and elsewhere. But if we're not careful it can limit our understanding.

The most serious problem with the audience metaphor is that it makes writing into a performance in front of "all those folks out there in chairs." Anthony Paré unpacks the metaphor:

The actor/writer image has a certain romantic richness and may complement the notion of "persona" in literary discourse, but between actor and audience is the proscenium arch and the imaginary "fourth wall" of the theatre. Actors on stage stare into the bright front-of-house lights and see only the dark, indistinct shape of a faceless crowd. It is true that good actors sense the audience, adjusting their performance by heeding the subtle cues of sound and silence, but the audience only responds, never initiates, and the relationship begins with curtain up and ends with curtain down. (Paré, 1991, p. 47)

The audience metaphor of writing can be limiting, then, to the extent that it turns readers into passive recipients, writers into actors, and writing into performance.

As Paré argues, associated with this performance view of writing are a number of assumptions—or, more precisely, misconceptions—about writer–reader relationships. The first misconception is that the writer–reader relationship is singular, one-to-one: Multiple readers of the same text form a monolithic, unitary entity called "the" audience. The second misconception is that the writer–reader relationship is temporary: The writer's relation with readers begins and ends with the text. The third misconception is that the writer–reader relationship is a one-way monologue: The writer speaks; passive readers listen.

WRITING IN THE WORKPLACE

All these notions are beginning to be challenged. The challenge is coming from compositionists like Paré who are studying writing not only in the academy, but in business, government, and professional settings. They are investigating, in Cooper's (1986) phrase, the "ecology of writing," and they are finding that writing is an inherently social and communal activity—much more social than terms like "audience" have led us to expect. In order to understand the new thinking about audience, let us follow these scholars and researchers into the workplace.[3]

Dorothy Winsor (1989) finds evidence for "the corporate construction of knowledge" in the writing of an automotive engineer. Against the Romantic ideal of the solitary, independent writer, Winsor and other scholars argue that writing in the workplace is necessarily a collaborative enterprise.

Collaborative writing at work doesn't just mean more than one person working on a report. It means that any individual's writing is called forth and shaped by the needs and aims of the organization, and that to be understood it must draw on vocabulary, knowledge, and beliefs other organization members share. Writing at work is firmly embedded in a social web. (Winsor, 1989, p. 271)

Writing in the workplace is "embedded in a social web" because written products must find a fit within the organization's objectives. Such objectives become known to individual worker-writers in part through a writing-editing-revising routine called *document cycling.* The term was coined by James Paradis, David Dobrin, and Richard Miller (1985), who studied the writing of scientists and engineers at Exxon ITD, a research and development company. In document cycling, a draft by a subordinate is read by the writer's supervisor; the supervisor's comments and criticisms are incorporated in the next draft; if satisfactory, this draft is passed up to the next level in the company hierarchy, where the cycle of reading, commenting, and revising continues.

Paradis, Dobrin, and Miller observed that supervisors use document cycling to establish leverage over the timing and substance of subordinates' work. By assigning a document, supervisors set work objectives, distribute tasks among staff members, and call work in when it is due. By reading the document, supervisors identify work that needs to be redone or extended (p. 294).

The concept of document cycling was elaborated by Rachel Spilka (1988), who also studied the writing of engineers. Spilka's model of document cycling illustrates the route a text might take as it progresses up the administrative ladder, becoming, in Winsor's terminology, ever more inscribed as corporate knowledge.[4] Correspondingly, the model shows which readers might see drafts of the document at different points in the composing-revising process (Spilka, 1988, p. 211).

Spilka's main concern, however, is to point out the diversity of writer–reader interactions in the workplace. As a result, a number of traditional assumptions about audience are upended. For instance, the engineers that Spilka studied all wrote to multiple readers, not to a single, unitary audience. Even though it was possible to divide the readers into "segments" (design specialists, software specialists, and so on), the engineers tended not to write different reports, or even different sections of reports, for different segments. Most writers tried to appeal to all segments of a multiple readership throughout their documents. Spilka (1988) refers indirectly to the diversity of readers when she points out the dangers of stereotyping. As we saw earlier, the traditional approach to audience requires that writers classify readers by occupation or role, and "aim" their writing accordingly. The problem is that occupation and role are poor. predictors of reading behavior. For instance, whereas conventional wisdom has it that managers read only the executive summary of a report, Spilka found that managers' reading is diverse: Different managers read different things (p. 218).

The diversity of writer–reader interactions described by Spilka brings us back to Paré (1991), who studied writing in the nonacademic setting of a social work agency in Montreal. The social workers, associated with the juvenile court system, were required to write "predisposition reports"— advisory reports to a judge concerning the sentencing of a juvenile found guilty of an offense under the criminal code. A given report, however, is read not only by the judge, but also by the juvenile, his or her family, and two lawyers, defense and prosecution; reports usually find their way into other agencies where they may be read by other social workers, psychiatrists, and so on. Paré interviewed social workers before, while, and after their reports were written.

Paré's work challenges all the assumptions, described earlier, associated with the traditional view of audience.

- Multiple readers of the same text do *not* form a monolithic audience. On the contrary, multiple readers have different motives for reading, bring different experiences to their reading, and have different attitudes to the subject and the writer. Paré's social workers wrote a single document, but it embodied diverse writer–reader relationships—with client, family, judge, defense lawyer, prosecution lawyer, other social workers, and so on. As one worker said, "I write with one pen and twenty hats" (p. 52).

- The writer–reader relationship is *not* a temporary one or limited to the text. Instead, a writer's relationship with readers "often exists prior to the text, changes during composing, and may be continued, altered, or ended by the text" (p. 51). The relationship between social workers and clients, or between social workers and judges, was not confined to writing and reading predisposition reports. This was only one part of the larger, ongoing interaction between them; for example, the social workers served as the juveniles' parole officers.

- The writer–reader relationship is *not* monologic, in which writers speak and readers listen. On the contrary, the writer–reader relationship is better described as a *dialogue*. The relationship is dialogic because even the simplest text is not complete until a reader responds. As reader-response theorists and others have argued, readers are not passive targets to be aimed at or empty vessels to be filled, but active participants who construct meaning at least as energetically as writers.[5] Furthermore, whereas monologue implies that writing involves only one voice at a time, dialogue suggests that texts always contain other voices, whether explicitly, through citation and paraphrase, or implicitly, through allusions and phrases that are "in the air" (Porter, 1986). Mikhail Bakhtin (1935/1981) observed that "our speech is filled to overflowing with other people's words" (p. 337); presumably the social workers' predisposition reports were filled to overflowing with conventional social work language, traces from previous reports, quotations and paraphrases of client and family, and so on.

In short, the implications of the audience metaphor—that writing is a performance and that writers "act" in front of passive listeners—are seriously challenged by studies of writing in the workplace. But if writer–reader relationships are inadequately represented by the audience metaphor, how can they be better understood?

A NEW METAPHOR: WRITING AS CONVERSATION

A number of social constructionist thinkers—notably Richard Rorty (1979) in philosophy and Kenneth Bruffee (1984) in composition—suggest a new metaphor. They propose that we think of writing as a dialogue or *conversation* that takes place within *communities of discourse*. The idea of human discourse as an ongoing conversation was expressed in a powerful image by Kenneth Burke.

Imagine that you enter a parlor. You come late. When you arrive, others have long preceded you, and they are engaged in a heated discussion, a discussion too heated for them to pause and tell you exactly what it is about. In fact, the discussion had already begun long before any of them got there, so that no one present is qualified to retrace for you all the steps that had gone before. You listen for a while, until you decide that you have caught the tenor of the argument; then you put in your oar. Someone answers; you answer him; another comes to your defense; another aligns himself against you, to either the embarrassment or gratification of your opponent, depending upon the quality of your ally's assistance. However, the discussion is interminable. The hour grows late, you must depart. And you do depart, with the discussion still vigorously in progress. (Burke, 1973, pp. 110–111)

Burke's parable helps us see texts not as performances, but as turns in an ongoing conversation. The conversation metaphor seems to express—in ways that the audience metaphor cannot—what was going on when Paré's social workers wrote predisposition reports. Thinking of the reports as turns in a conversation helps us see that they are interactional: They are speech acts that modify the relationships between writers and their various readers. Thinking of the reports as turns helps us see, as well, that they are not self-contained, but instead are moments in an ongoing process that both precedes and follows the documents themselves. From the perspective of the conversational model, texts are not messages delivered to audiences, but utterances "shaped by the relationships, concerns, and procedures of the community" (Paré, 1991, p. 51).

Conversations in the Academy

Perhaps it's clear enough that predisposition reports—as well as letters, memos, and other genres of business and technical communication—are forms of interaction, but what about scholarly and scientific articles? Academic writing is usually considered a matter of information and logic, not social interaction. The conversation metaphor, however, helps us understand how academic writers, as much as any others, are involved in multiple relationships, both with readers and with other writers.

Academic writers are multiply connected to their readers because readers do not constitute a single mass "audience" but rather a diverse collection of individuals, each with their own purposes and interests. Thus the writer–reader relationship is not one-to-one (writer–audience), but one-to-many (writer–readers). There are other kinds of relations at stake, as well. Writers must consider the relationships between themselves and other writers. Furthermore—and, as Paré (1992) observes, "completely obscured by the audience metaphor" (p. 53)—they must consider the relationships various readers have with one another, as well as relationships between readers and other writers.

The intensely social, interactional nature of academic writing is especially obvious in the elaborate systems of quotation, citation, and paraphrase that have evolved.[6] Writers quote, cite, and paraphrase so that they might, as Burke says, "align" themselves with and against other writers. Paré writes:

The use of other people's words or ideas in text is often a way of establishing alliances or oppositions with individual readers or groups. Attribution, use of quotations, and referencing are all methods of establishing, altering, and maintaining relationships within discourse communities. When, in academic discourse, we use another's criticism of a community member, rather than being critical ourselves, we often do so to preserve our relationships. (Paré, 1991, pp. 54–55)

Understanding academic writing as a form of conversation helps us understand the crucial role that discourse communities play in enabling and constraining texts.[7] The term *community*, incidentally, should not be taken to imply cozy like-mindedness. As Joseph Harris (1989) argues, it may be better to think of a "city" of discourses, rather than a discourse community, because "city" implies diversity and competing practices: "The metaphor of the city would also allow us to view a certain amount of change and struggle within a community not as threats to its coherence but as normal activity" (p. 20). Similarly, the conversation metaphor itself is limited if it connotes only fireside chats among good friends. John Trimbur (1989) writes that only in "the dream of conversation as perfect dialogue" is there complete reciprocity and mutual recognition (p. 612); actual conversations, we know, are governed by power relations that determine who may speak and what may be said. Thus, community and conversation are valuable metaphors, but they should not be sentimentalized.

With that warning in mind, we see that the concept of discourse community is valuable precisely because it draws attention to the social contexts of academic writing. In contrast, according to the audience metaphor, writers determine their content independently of readers; writers decide what to say, and only then decide how to accommodate the message to a particular readership. In the conversation metaphor, however, it is the writer's discourse community that enables or calls forth the contribution in the first place. Every act of writing (to invoke Burke's image again) is an act of joining a conversation already in progress. Therefore every act of writing must be relevant, or be seen as relevant, to the conversation it aspires to join. For example, psychologists who wish to say something about schizophrenia will have to find a way into the conversation that has been going on for many years in books and journals. More to the point, they won't have anything to say about schizophrenia unless they have been attending to this conversation. "Content" grows out of and contributes to the ongoing discussion.

It may be misleading, then, to advise writers to determine their content and purpose *before* defining their audience. (Recall that for Bond and Magistrale, 1987, audience is the third decision psychology writers are advised to make, after subject and purpose.) On the contrary, it is one's audience or discourse community with its projects and agendas that motivates inquiry in the first place (Bartholomae, 1985). This primary role of audience was recognized in classical rhetoric, where writing was seen to begin with the identification of a *stasis*, the precise question about which writer and audience were in disagreement (Gage, 1981). As John Gage (1981) writes, "Before they come together, an audience and a writer each know something already about matters that interest them mutually, and it is the difference between what they know that motivates the need for communication—in both directions—and which therefore compels the act of writing itself" (pp. 1–2). Thus, far from being a relatively late decision, one's "audience"—interpreted more broadly as "discourse community"—actually enables academic writing. Only because the audience is already there, asking the same questions, interested in the same issues, do inquiry and writing occur.

If discourse communities enable writing by making available certain topics, however, they also constrain it. Certain topics are currently on the floor, but, just as surely, others are not. Modern-day psychologists may be able to join conversations on schizophrenia and artificial intelligence, but they will have trouble holding the floor to talk about drive theory in Hull's sense or genetic psychology in Hall's. Those discussions are essentially finished, at least for the time being.

Readers' Role in Determining Meaning

This is not to say, however, that you cannot write against the grain, violating or frustrating community expectations. The question is, Will you be heard? By phrasing the question this way, the conversation metaphor directs our attention away from the written text and toward the readers who are responsible for its reception. This point bears some explanation.

According to the audience metaphor, what seems most relevant to writing is the quality of the text: its clarity, logic, coherence. It is assumed, at least implicitly, that the meaning or point of the writing is in the text; texts carry meaning from author to audience (Reddy, 1979). The conversation metaphor, on the other hand, redirects attention to the reception or uptake of a text—how readers interpret and use it. In this view, a piece of writing doesn't "have" a single meaning; its various meanings are the different ways readers take it.

For some enlightenment on this issue, let us briefly step outside the boundaries of rhetoric and composition studies. Sociologists of science argue that readers of a scientific text play a decisive role in determining its meanings. Whereas the "audience" for a scientific article may suggest a relatively passive entity, "readers" are anything but. Karin Knorr-Cetina (1981) notes that "the readers of [a] published paper dissect and contest the text . . . ; they believe some arguments, disbelieve others, qualify some claims as warranted and others not, and cast a web of interpretations and relevances upon the bare words" (p. 107). A text may be stabilized in print when it is published, but what is not stabilized is its meaning. This, Knorr-Cetina argues, is up for grabs, to be "redefined, modified, [or] analogically transformed" by readers, or, alternatively, to be "criticised and rejected" (p. 131).

Similarly, Bruno Latour (1987) argues that scientific facts are not, as the audience model seems to suggest, made by individual scientist-writers. Rather, fact making is necessarily a social, collective enterprise. Scientists may advance knowledge claims, but in themselves these claims are not much better than wishes. Only if later writers treat the claim as a fact will it become one. Thus the fate of any given knowledge claim or scientific statement—the decision about whether it is a fact or an artifact—"depends on a sequence of debates later on" (p. 27). Like genes, scientific statements survive only if they "manage to pass themselves on to later bodies" (p. 38).

In summary, the conversation metaphor helps us see, as the audience metaphor does not, the crucial roles that discourse communities and readers play in psychological writing. Discourse communities enable and constrain texts, while readers determine their meanings.

Real Readers

The readers who determine meaning are not the faceless, passive beings that "audience" seems to suggest. *Real readers* are the active, flesh-and-blood people who actually engage a piece of writing.

In the workplace, of course, it is not hard to appreciate the reality of readers. Here the reader of your memo is not some demographic abstraction, but is very likely the person down the hall. For example, the engineer whose technical report is cycled through levels of the company's hierarchy often knows who will be reading the document, and when, and may even be able to predict what they will say. At Exxon ITD, the senior-level writers, especially, tend to know who their readers are and what they want: "They were writing to real people, whom they often knew by first name. This makes a difference" (Paradis, Dobrin, & Miller, 1985, p. 303).

In academic settings, readers may be less visible but they are no less real. One important class of real reader is the writer's colleagues and supervisors, whose comments and criticisms often shape the text in powerful but unseen ways. We may learn the names of these "enablers" in the acknowledgments section, but we seldom learn the true extent of their influence (LeFevre, 1987, p. 30; Pittenger, 1986).

Undoubtedly all academic writers are used to getting comments and suggestions from others before submitting a draft for publication. I was familiar with this process, too; but, even so, I didn't fully appreciate the significance of readers until just a few years ago. After Russ Hunt and I had drafted an article, we asked three colleagues for comments and criticisms. They responded by noting problems with organization, suggesting new references and metaphors, and pointing out grammatical and typographical errors. But most important, one of them, Alan Mason, convinced us that the knowledge claim we were trying to advance was more appropriate to a social science conversation than to the literary one we had in mind. As a result of Al's comments, we recast the article, eventually sending it to a different journal from the one first planned. The point is that our readers were also, in an important sense, *coauthors* who collaborated with us in writing the article. (This episode is described more fully by Reither & Vipond, 1989.)

In our case, the readers were "trusted assessors" (Mullins, 1973)—friends who could be counted on to help us write the most convincing paper possible. But Hunt and I were free to ignore their suggestions, and often we did. In other cases, writers cannot reject their readers' advice so easily. For example, in scientific research institutes—just as in the organizations and workplaces described previously—it is common practice for a draft by a junior scientist to be cycled through levels of the institutional hierarchy. If they wish to keep their jobs, such scientist-writers are required to revise their papers according to the comments of supervisors. Knorr-Cetina (1981, chap. 5) shows how this can result in tension if not outright hostility between writers and critics; she describes one draft of a scientific paper as showing "a whole battle of annotations" (p. 106).

Although they don't necessarily experience it as a battle, all writers encounter the revision process when they send a manuscript to a journal. Now, though, the readers who suggest or demand changes are not colleagues or supervisors but journal editors and referees, playing the role of disciplinary representatives or gatekeepers. Greg Myers (1990) describes the changes that two biology papers underwent in the course of being submitted to and rejected by a series of scientific journals. Myers's work illustrates the *negotiation* process in which authors and reviewers try to reach agreement on the value and scope of a particular knowledge claim. Not surprisingly, the writers wanted to claim greater significance than the reviewers were willing to grant. The negotiations did not concern the technical merits of the papers so much as their "appropriateness" for a given publication outlet. The biologist-writers were eventually able to get their articles published, but they had to settle for less prestigious, more specialized journals than the ones originally envisioned.

Myers's work, along with Knorr-Cetina's and Reither's and mine, suggests that forms of document cycling are practiced in the academy as much as in the workplace. Just as business organizations use document cycling to ensure that individual work advances corporate objectives, academic discourse communities—biology, psychology, and so on—use it to ensure that work meets disciplinary goals and standards.

Notice that in all these instances of document cycling it was real readers, not "audiences," who were involved. A comparable situation exists in educational settings, where we meet yet other forms of cycling. For example, the problem faced by the prototypical graduate student in psychology is not how to persuade her "audience." The problem is how to revise her thesis now that she has three sets of comments from committee members, each of whom has different—and to some extent, conflicting—interests and commitments. (These readers may be all too real.)

The graduate student's dilemma illustrates an essential point. Real readers do not necessarily respond to writing with utter detachment and objectivity. The Myth of the General Reader is widespread—in psychology handbooks, as we have seen, and even in those areas of composition still in the grip of "current-traditional" thinking. Writers who have had a manuscript rejected may think differently, but meanwhile the handbooks present a world in which, as Sharon Crowley (1990) puts it, "readers always react objectively and fairly to any piece of writing no matter who its author, what thesis she presents, or what subject she chooses" (p. 161). But how likely is it, for instance, that a "pro-life" reader will respond enthusiastically to a study that finds psychological benefits of abortion?

Real readers are seldom the rational, passive beings that terms like "audience" and "the general reader" imply. How, or even whether, a given text is read depends on readers' motives for reading, their relations to the writer, and their attitudes to the subject. "Audience" silences and makes invisible these readers. By doing so, it implies that writing takes place in a separate, virtual realm well removed from the real world of actual readers and social relationships. In their writing, academics may pretend that they do not have relationships with their readers and other writers, but they do. Established writers, at least, do not just *cite* other writers, they *know* them "through real social encounters" (Cooper, 1986, p. 372). Like the managers at Exxon, established academic writers often know one another by first name; they meet one another at conferences; they exchange preprints and e-mail.

The pretense that scholarly writing is separate from the daily world collapses when you find yourself criticizing the views of someone who happens to be a friend, colleague, or thesis adviser. For example, in the Comment/Response section of *College English* (October 1990), Maxine Hairston and John Trimbur seem to need to acknowledge their real-world relationship before they can get down to the academic business at hand, which is critique.

Hairston: "I like John and I'm interested in his topic, but . . . " (Hairston, 1990, p. 695).

Trimbur: "Finally, to Maxine Hairston, I must say, for sure, that I like you too. But you already knew that. What worries me is the charge . . . " (Trimbur, 1990, p. 699).

Closer to home, this is how B. F. Skinner (1977) responded to an article by Richard Herrnstein: "When one has published nine books setting forth a scientific position, it is disconcerting to find it misunderstood. To be misunderstood by a former student and present colleague is especially puzzling" (p. 1006). As I read it, there is something poignant in Skinner's

characterization of Herrnstein as "a former student and present colleague"—someone whose office, in fact, was next to his (Skinner, 1983,
p. 374). Whether Skinner experienced Herrnstein's paper more as betrayal
than as criticism, I don't know; according to Skinner they remained
friends. The point is that they had far more than a "writer–audience"
relationship with each other.

SUMMARY

In this chapter I have drawn on composition studies to develop a new
understanding of writer–reader relationships in psychology. The practical
implications of such understanding, I believe, mainly concern how we
present writing to our students: Do we have students write for anonymous
audiences, or do we invite them into the ongoing conversations of the
field? Discussion of such questions, however, will be deferred until
Chapter 5.

Meanwhile, a renewed understanding of writer–reader relationships in
psychology can also affect how we think of the discipline itself. As
suggested throughout this chapter, the audience metaphor encourages a
view of writing as performance. But performance is a limiting notion, not
only because of its monologic implications (active writer, passive reader),
but because it implies that a discipline is a series of discrete contributions.
Performance puts the emphasis on individual actors—the "great person"
theory of history—rather than on communally provided investigative and
interpretive practices in writing and knowing.

At one level, admittedly, understanding writing as conversation instead
of performance is merely replacing one metaphor with another. But the
conversation metaphor redirects our attention, allowing us to see what may
have been indistinct before. First, it helps us transcend the active/passive
dichotomy; in a dialogue it is the listener who enables the contribution and
whose response is crucial to its meaning. Second, revisioning psychology
as conversation and dialogue helps us see the discipline as a "Burkean
parlor"—as an ongoing, language-based activity in which, nevertheless,
topics can and do change abruptly. The new metaphors help us see
psychology as a discourse community—or, even better, as a city of
discourses—rather than as a scientific edifice built with bricks of truth and
fact. Third, whereas "audience" perpetuates the myth of uniformity, recognizing the multiplicity of writer–reader (and other) relationships in
psychology opens a space for understanding alternative and competing
discourses, the subject of Chapter 3.

Chapter Three

The Genre Question
in Psychology

Arguments that any currently privileged set of stylistic conventions of academic discourse are inherently better—even that any currently privileged set of intellectual practices are better for scholarship or for thinking or for arguing or for rooting out self-deception—such arguments seem problematic now.

—Peter Elbow (1991, p. 153)

"Genders of Writing," the title of an article by David Bleich (1989), seems at first to be a misprint. After all, the usual term for different kinds of writing is not *gender* but *genre*. But Bleich's pun is his way of emphasizing that to classify anything—in this case, kinds of writing—is always in part a political gesture. The pun is also, he says, a way of emphasizing Gerda Lerner's (1986) idea that gender categories are historically prior to such other categories as race and class. Moreover—and, from my point of view, most important—the pun emphasizes that what has been called "official academic discourse" supports the traditional sex/gender system (Bleich, 1989, p. 14).

In his article Bleich explores academic writing from a feminist perspective. He uses Ralph Cohen's work on genre to underscore some points about gender. Cohen aims to rescue the concept of genre from its usual role as a static taxonomy. For Cohen, genre is dynamic. The different kinds of writing that we recognize now—novels, plays, scientific reports, and so on—are indeed different categories, but the categories are not fixed.

Genres are human constructions and are therefore understood differently in different social and historical circumstances. As Bleich (1989) puts it, "every work of literature [and, I would add, science] is both a text and a kind of text and . . . the relationship between a text and how we identify it is historically and culturally determined" (p. 14). For example, texts originally considered "science" or "history" may at some later time be considered "literature."[1]

As well as being variable across time and place, genres are internally mixed. Clifford Geertz (1983) uses the term *genre blurring* to refer to the tendency in modern intellectual life for discourse types to merge, blend, and overlap.

The present jumbling of varieties of discourse has grown to the point where it is becoming difficult either to label authors (What *is* Foucault—historian, philosopher, political theorist? What Thomas Kuhn—historian, philosopher, sociologist of knowledge?) or to classify works. . . . It is a phenomenon general enough and distinctive enough to suggest that what we are seeing is not just another redrawing of the cultural map—the moving of a few disputed borders, the marking of some more picturesque mountain lakes—but an alteration of the principles of mapping. Something is happening to the way we think about the way we think. (Geertz, 1983, p. 20)

Genres, in Cohen's view, are *always* blurred, jumbled, mixed, or combinatory; pure genres do not exist. At any moment in history a single genre is made up of various others. Mixed genres are the norm because whenever there are borders—between countries or between genres—there are border crossings. Texts cross borders for social and economic reasons, just as people do. For Cohen, the upshot is that genre naming—and, Bleich adds significantly, gender naming—"is inevitably both necessary and loose" (quoted by Bleich, 1989, p. 15). Genres and genders are not facts of nature, but historical and cultural practices.

Other composition scholars would agree with Cohen and Bleich that genres are social practices rather than rigid classificatory types. For example, Carolyn Miller (1984) argues that genres should be defined in terms of the "social action" they are used to accomplish (p. 151). Charles Bazerman (1988) points out that the features of a particular genre are a "solution to a problem in social interaction" (p. 62). John Swales (1990) emphasizes that members of a given genre share a set of "communicative purposes" (p. 58). Graham Smart (1993) argues that genres are distinctive profiles of regularities across the dimensions of texts, composing processes, and reading practices. And Richard Coe (1987) considers genres and other types of rhetorical structures to be a kind of "social memory" (p. 19).

Coe's study of genre—or, more generally, *form*—is especially interesting, I believe, because he makes the case that genre is *heuristic*. As mentioned earlier, form has traditionally been viewed as a collection of inert categories (novels, poems, scientific papers, and so on). Coe notes that the underlying metaphor here is that of form as a "container" into which one places or pours one's "content." Against this view, Coe argues for a conception of form as process, as *form-ing*. Meaning is not poured into ready-made containers; instead, subject matter becomes meaningful only when given shape or form. Meaning and form are therefore interdependent, and in this sense, form can be seen as heuristic.

Form, in its emptiness, is heuristic, for it guides a structured search. Faced with the emptiness of a form, a *human* being seeks matter to fill it. Form becomes, therefore, a motive for generating information. Like any heuristic, it motivates a search for information of a certain type: when the searchers can anticipate what shape of stuff they seek, generation is less free, but much more efficient; by constraining the search, form directs attention. (Coe, 1987, p. 18)

Thus, for example, the form of the empirical report directs psychologist-writers to search for information concerning methods, materials, participants, procedures, results, and so on. This form is what Coe would call a "shaped emptiness" that motivates writers of psychology to search for and generate certain types of information. Indeed, knowing that they will be "writing up" their results according to a certain formal pattern, psychologists may design their research to con-form to it. In this way, form can direct practice as well as attention.

By directing attention *to* certain types of information, forms necessarily direct it away from other types. Any given form makes it more difficult to recognize or discover information that doesn't fit. A particular message may be difficult or even impossible to communicate within a conventional form. When form constrains or blocks messages that are contrary to the interests of some powerful group, it can serve an ideological function. "Insofar as form guides function," Coe (1987) writes, "formal values may carry implicit moral/political values" (p. 20).

What has all this to do with psychology? At the very least, the discussion of genre in composition studies and elsewhere can sensitize psychologists to the diversity of genres in our discipline and the extent to which they are blurred. Beyond that, the discussion alerts us to the heuristic function of genre. As Coe suggests, a particular form enables certain kinds of meanings to be discovered and communicated; at the same time, it disables others. Furthermore, because genre is heuristic it can serve ideological and political functions, and in this sense the genre question in psychology needs to be understood as a gender question as well. As we will see later, according to the feminist critique offered by Bleich and others, official academic discourse, committed as it is to an ethic of competition, suffers from a masculinist bias.

I would like to start, though, by examining the range and blurring of genres in psychology. Then I will consider characteristics of—and finally, alternatives to—"official academic discourse."

RECOGNIZING THE RANGE OF GENRES IN PSYCHOLOGY

For a preliminary list of genres in psychology, we can begin with the ones listed in the American Psychological Association's *Publication Manual* (third edition, 1983). Concerned, understandably, only with articles published in APA journals, the *Manual* recognizes three main types: (1) reports of empirical studies; (2) review articles; and (3) theoretical articles. At first the three genres appear to be of equal weight, as the *Manual* describes each in a separate paragraph (p. 21). No more is said about review and theoretical articles, however, whereas a further eight pages are devoted to empirical reports. The message is unmistakable that the empirical report is or should be the dominant kind of writing in psychology.

Of even lower status than review and theoretical articles are other, miscellaneous types of writing occasionally published in APA journals: brief reports, case histories, comments and replies, discussions of quantitative methods, and monographs (p. 21).[2]

The *Manual* doesn't mention books, but it is estimated that as much as thirty percent of scholarly writing in psychology now appears in book form (Granick, 1989). Edited collections, in particular, are becoming increasingly popular (Foss, 1985).[3] Lois Granick (1989) observes that the chapters of such edited books often report new data; in general these chapters "closely resemble a long journal article" (p. ix). On the other hand, special issues of journals are often indistinguishable from edited books. In short, the lines separating "chapter," "article," "book," and "journal" are becoming increasingly blurred.

As noted in Chapter 1, *Contemporary Psychology*, APA's book review journal, receives approximately 3,000 books per year, of which sixty percent or so are reviewed (Harvey, 1992, 1993). This suggests that

English-writing psychologists are publishing books at the rate of about eight per day, and—not incidentally—that the book review itself is a neglected genre of writing in the discipline.

In addition to edited collections, there are other kinds of scholarly, semischolarly, and nonscholarly books; other genres, not necessarily in book form, shade into journalism and popular culture. Consider these, for example: handbooks, textbooks, reference manuals; newspaper articles, popularizations (as in *Scientific American* or *Psychology Today*), psychology journalism (the *APA Monitor*, or the Canadian Psychological Association's *Psynopsis*); and the countless newsletters and information sheets that smaller groups publish. Not to mention those "oracles at the supermarket" (Starker, 1989): paperback self-help books sold at the checkout counter. As all these examples suggest, it is impossible in practice to draw clear, unequivocal lines between what is and is not "psychological discourse."

Unpublished Genres

None of the above listings even begins to tap all the unpublished genres of writing that psychologists engage in, whether they work in applied or academic settings: letters of recommendation, assessments of clients and programs, case studies, grant proposals, progress reports, memos, journal and grant referee reports, course descriptions and syllabi, lectures and lecture notes, exam questions, lab notes, technical reports, computer network contributions and e-mail, conference papers and posters, marginalia. And psychology students write essays, exams, term papers, literature reviews, and proposals; they "write down" observations and lecture notes and "write up" experiments, theses, and dissertations (Darville, quoted by Kirby & McKenna, 1989, p. 18). Thus the range of genres in psychology is greater than we usually think.[4]

Examples of Mixed Genres

Cohen may be right that all genres are mixed, but in psychology some are radically and deliberately mixed. Consider, for example, the genre blurring in "Hail to the Chiefs," where Harvey Mindess (1975) presents a synoptic history of psychology in verse; in "Learning Theory," where James McConnell (1961) describes operant conditioning chambers, mazes, and jumping stands in the language of science fiction; or in *Freud's Own Cookbook*, where James Hillman and Charles Boer (1985) present psychoanalytic lore and real recipes in about equal proportions. But probably the best known instance of blurred genres in psychology is B. F. Skinner's *Walden Two* (1948)—an argument about behaviorism in the form of a utopian novel.[5]

Two other works that illustrate the range of genres in psychology may be briefly described. Richard Nisbett's (1990) "Anticreativity Letters: Advice from a Senior Tempter to a Junior Tempter" purports to be a discussion about how to inhibit psychologists' creativity. Modeled on C. S. Lewis's *Screwtape Letters*, "The Anticreativity Letters" is actually Nisbett's way of suggesting how to stimulate creative scientific work. Genres are deliberately mixed by George Howard (1989) in *A Tale of Two Stories: Excursions into a Narrative Approach to Psychology*. In alternating chapters, Howard presents autobiography ("A Story of George") and history of science ("A Story of Science"). The book's structure and breezy style challenge conventional notions of psychological writing. Notice, finally, that both Nisbett and Howard use literary models for their writing: C. S. Lewis and Charles Dickens, respectively.

But in spite of the wide range of genres and clear evidence of genre blurring, it is still the case that in psychology there is one dominant genre: the empirical report. Judging from the prominence given empirical reports by the APA *Manual*, it is apparent that all other genres—to some extent, even theoretical and review articles—are considered secondary or derivative forms. Thus, when one speaks of "writing like a psychologist," what is usually meant is writing empirical reports. Undergraduate honors' theses are typically empirical reports, and certainly one of the most important (w)rites of passage for graduate students is completion of a thesis or dissertation—genres closely related to the empirical report (Swales, 1990, chap. 8).[6] All this suggests that in our discipline the empirical report is privileged.

Nevertheless, theory/review articles, essays, and books seem to have at least as much impact in psychology as empirical reports. Different methods have been used to determine the most important works and the most influential journals. Although any method is imperfect, it is interesting that no matter what is used—citation counts, appearances in textbooks, subjective ratings—the results show that the most influential journals are those publishing theory/review articles and essays, not empirical reports. For example, among APA journals, *Psychological Review*, *Psychological Bulletin*, and *American Psychologist* appear to have the most influence.[7] Similarly, in at least two subdisciplines—cognitive psychology and perception—studies indicate that the most highly cited work is in the form of books, chapters, and theory/review articles (White, 1983, 1987).[8]

None of this is meant to suggest that empirical reports aren't extremely valuable. Empirical reports have played and will continue to play a crucial role in advancing knowledge claims in psychology. Without empirical reports to summarize and interpret, many theory/review articles and books would never have been written. Thus, I am not questioning the value of empirical reports as such, but rather the *hierarchy* of genres that necessarily places empirical reports above all other work. Do empirical reports have a monopoly on psychological truth and wisdom?

I suggest that we resist thinking about the genres of psychology as a rigid vertical structure organized according to value (empirical reports at the top, marginalia at the bottom), and instead—as composition specialists tend to—think of genre as *practice*, that is, in terms of the different purposes, readers, and occasions associated with writing. Then perhaps we can see the extent to which conventional forms direct attention to certain types of information and knowledge, thereby deflecting it from other types. I suggest, too, that psychologists bear in mind Cohen's point that genres are both "necessary" and "loose." The concept of kinds of writing is clearly useful—provided we remember that the kinds tend to be mixed, overlapping, and blurred.

ACADEMIC WRITING

In the present hierarchy of psychological genres, empirical reports are the highest ranking member. Now I would like to blur the distinctions between these various genres, classifying them all as *psychological academic discourse*. In some ways, academic writing in psychology differs from that of biology, philosophy, composition studies, and so on.[9] But if these differences, too, are blurred, what we have then is *generic academic discourse*—"the discourse that academics use when they publish for other academics" (Elbow, 1991, p. 135). What does academic discourse *do*? In Peter Elbow's (1990) words, "[it] makes arguments, solves problems, analyzes texts and issues, tries to answer hard questions—and usually refers to and builds on other academic discourse" (p. 7). Elbow and other commentators claim that there is something characteristic about academic discourse, something that distinguishes it from "nonacademic" writing. For the rest of this chapter I will discuss the characteristics and problems of academic discourse, especially as they have been identified by composition scholars. An important assumption is that academic writing in psychology shares many if not all the features (and problems) of academic writing in general.

A number of composition scholars have joined the conversation on academic writing. Olivia Frey (1990, p. 509) offers a list of distinctive features. In academic discourse, she says, emphasis is on the finished product, with little or no reference to the processes by which the product was created. Related to this is a preference for impersonal, "objective" knowledge over personal experience. Knowledge that is considered true for all places and times is valued above local, situated knowing. Academic writing, Frey says, is constructed in terms of hierarchies rather than networks of relationships; it relies more heavily on the "either/or" than on the "both/and."

Other characteristics are noted by Elbow (1991). His argument is that academic discourse teaches a set of social and authority relations. By using formal language, jargon, and complex syntax, academics are saying both that they are "professionals" and that they do not encourage discussion with nonprofessionals (p. 146). (As an example, Elbow cites Bruno Bettelheim's 1984 argument that the English-speaking medical community mistranslated Freud's everyday German words into obscure, exclusionary Latin terms: *id*, *ego*, *superego*.) Exclusionary writing sends the message, "We don't want to talk to you or hear from you unless you use our language" (Elbow, 1991, p. 147).

Many of the foregoing characteristics can be summed up by saying that, in academic writing, reasons and evidence count for more than feelings, opinions, or experiences. As Elbow says, academic writers have a praiseworthy goal: to be clear about claims and assertions rather than just insinuating or implying them. In academic discourse, thinking "stands on its own two feet" rather than leaning on the authority of the writer or the fit with its readers (p. 140).

Nevertheless, Elbow goes on to say that this notion of academic discourse rests on a number of problematic assumptions. Is it possible to separate reasons and arguments from the person who holds them? Are there such things as "unheld" opinions—assertions *not* influenced by who says and hears them? Aren't our "intellectual" positions always influenced by our feelings, class, race, gender, sexual orientation, and historical position? Does thinking ever "stand on its own two feet"?

As I read him, Elbow is saying that the problem with academic discourse is that it pretends not to be discourse, where *discourse* means "always talking to someone" (p. 140), "always located in a person speaking and an audience listening" (p. 141).

The very thing that is attractive and appealing about academic discourse is inherently problematic and perplexing. It tries to peel away from messages the evidence of how those messages are situated as the center of personal, political, or cultural interest; its conventions tend toward the sound of reasonable, disinterested, perhaps even objective (shall I say it?) men. (Elbow, 1991, p. 141)

Academic Discourse as Competition

The work of Frey and Elbow is helpful in pointing out some general attributes of academic writing. Now let's turn to a feature that has been identified as a defining characteristic by many commentators, namely, an "adversarial" or "competitive" quality. In "Sexism in Academic Styles of Learning," Bleich (1990) suggests that academic writing has the "habit" of adversarial reasoning. As luck would have it, one of Bleich's examples is an article by James Reither and myself (1989) in which we discuss different types of collaboration in writing. Reither and I argue that *collaborative* is a more useful term than *social*, in part because there are so many competing notions of what "social" might mean. But Bleich objects to our characterizing the different meanings of social as "competing." Why, he asks, this routine assumption of competition? The answer is "that is the way scholarly work is done" (Bleich, 1990, p. 241). Even to us Bleich's point seems well taken.

In order to justify new work on a topic, graduate students are trained—some would say "forced"—to review the literature and say why it is inadequate; new work can only be done if others have "failed to note" it. Alternatively, new work is done assuming that there is one whole truth and that various scholars are busy assembling all the pieces. . . . What is hard to find is . . . scholarship that does not seem to be participating in either the truth or power sweepstakes. (Bleich, 1990, pp. 241–242)

Janice Moulton's (1983) work, although focused on philosophical writing, draws attention to the competitiveness of academic discourse in general. Moulton suggests that philosophy is constrained by its reliance on the *adversary method* of reasoning—a paradigm in which opposing thinkers "try to defend their own views against counterexamples and produce counterexamples to opposing views" (p. 153). Rules of the contest prohibit mutual evaluation of premises; each thinker is required to accept the premises of the other, even if erroneous. The argument then proceeds by the strict rules of deductive logic until one side refutes (defeats) the other.

The adversary method is not limited to philosophy, however. In one form or another, it is the paradigm of choice throughout the humanities and, as we will see, in the sciences as well. Frey (1990) concludes that it is the default option in literary criticism. Like Bleich, she notes that literary critics establish the merit of their own ideas in part by discrediting the ideas of others; not infrequently, they resort to sarcasm and condescension to do so. Academic discourse is often played as a zero-sum game in which it is taken for granted that, in order for you to be right, others must be wrong.

If academic discourse is a game, it is one that students are expected to learn how to play, or suffer the consequences. In "No Exit: A Play of Literacy and Gender," Don Kraemer (1990) describes how a student named Flo failed the exit exam in his composition course because she was unable or unwilling to play the academic discourse game of competing against other writers. Kraemer's own view was that Flo should have passed the exam because she had given a competent summary of the writer's text; however, he was overruled by two outside examiners. In the academic discourse game, it's not enough to do what Flo did: stand on the sidelines, cheering other texts. We must play them, compete with them.

Competition and Antagonism in Scientific Discourse

In case the examples so far seem to suggest that competitive academic discourse is limited to composition studies and the humanities—and therefore none of this applies to us—let us turn briefly to academic discourse as practiced in psychology and other sciences. Psychologists, too, it seems, can be competitive, antagonistic, and sometimes just plain nasty.

For example, in the Point/Counterpoint section of *Contemporary Psychology*, which "invites discussion of reviews and of books reviewed," reviewers and authors alike sometimes drift from legitimate scholarly critique to verbal assaults. Thus reviewers may say that a book is "filled with arbitrary and gratuitous, not to mention irrelevant, statements" (LaBarbera & Blanchard, 1992, p. 1106), characterize an author's response as "verbal shenanigans" and "a new low in scholarship" (Valencia, 1992a, p. 505), or find a criticism "silly" (Valencia, 1992b, p. 505) and a strategy "unprofessional" (p. 504). For their part, authors may describe reviewers' work as "awkward and misleading" (Cohen, Montague, Nathanson, & Swerdlik, 1992a, p. 504) or "superficial and rambling" (Wittrock & Farley, 1992, p. 963); they may suggest that reviewers make "unfounded and lame statements" and "frivolous" criticisms, hold "idiosyncratic notions from an alien perspective" (Cohen, Montague, Nathanson, & Swerdlik, 1992a,

p. 504), or have "obvious deficiencies in . . . breadth and depth of knowledge" (Cohen, Montague, Nathanson, & Swerdlik, 1992b, p. 505).[10]

Thus, as Jane Tompkins (1988) suggests, the moral universe of academia does not appear vastly different from that of Rambo and Dirty Harry and their fans: "Violence takes place in the conference rooms at scholarly meetings and in the pages of professional journals" (p. 589). In a similar vein, Bruno Latour (1987) speaks of scientific practices, including writing, in terms of military metaphors. For Latour, science is fought on an agonistic field. It is a matter of force, struggle, strategy and tactics, balances of power, alliances; ultimately it is a matter of winning and losing. In the sciences as in the humanities, then, the underlying metaphor appears to be "argument is war" (Lakoff & Johnson, 1980).

Needless to say, this battlefield rhetoric has not gone unnoticed or unchallenged in the feminist critique of science. Evelyn Fox Keller (1985) says that some scientific methods entail "a kind of aggression that reflects a basic adversarial relation to the objects of study" (p. 123).

Problems, for many scientists, are to be "attacked," "conquered," or "licked." If subtler means fail, one resorts to "brute force," to the "hammer and tongs" approach. Even in gentler discourse, where problems are merely to be "solved," the underlying assumption is that in their solution, they will disappear; the process is perceived as one of clearing the field of obstacles. The complementary notion that the goal of solving problems is to reveal new questions, new perspectives, new understanding, may also be present but is considerably less in evidence. (Keller, 1985, pp. 123–124)[11]

Some Problems with Discourse as Competition

Keller's point that a reason for solving problems is to reveal "new questions, new perspectives, new understanding" suggests that a preoccupation with competition can place limits on knowledge itself. Understanding may be slowed or blocked entirely if one's only concern is to carry the day.

Thus the adversary method in philosophy has been criticized because it doesn't allow opposing thinkers to evaluate their premises together: The rules of deductive logic force you to accept whatever premises your opponent makes. Furthermore, as Moulton points out, oppositional logic means that much time is wasted subjecting positions to extreme tests (for example, proving the existence of a concept—the most extreme test of all) rather than showing the importance of an idea by demonstrating its fit with other ideas. You are allowed to ask, Is this argument valid?—but not, Is it important? Moulton is saying that, even though claims and arguments are always part of larger systems of ideas, you can't, within the adversary paradigm, opt out of the counterexample game to show how other premises and other data support an alternate system of ideas.[12]

Because adversarial thinking is focused on the local goal of winning the argument, its chances of achieving communal goals are much reduced. What is missing from adversarial thinking is, in Kenneth Burke's (1950) phrase, a spirit of "co-operative competition" in which the views of individual thinkers can be transcended (p. 203). By contrast, conventional academic discourse—immersed in competition in the narrow sense— lacks this communal dimension; it therefore "loses its social bearings" (Bleich, 1989, p. 18).[13]

Finally, Bleich suggests that the desire to establish universally valid arguments prevents academic writers from including personal experience. If personal experience were included, it might show, correctly, that a given idea is not universally but only "locally" valid, in a particular historical and cultural situation.

Despite its limitations, academic discourse continues to dominate writing in the disciplines. Bleich's contribution in "Genders of Writing" is to connect the idea of dominant genres with the better known idea of a dominant gender. The feminist critique asserts that the characteristics of academic writing that we have been discussing are by no means gender neutral. The orientation toward competition, rules, and "universal" truths are all consistent with what has been described by Bleich and other feminists as culturally masculine ways of knowing.

SCIENCE AND SEXISM

But why does academic discourse reflect masculine values? For Bleich (1989) the answer is that men have held and hold "all authoritative social roles . . .—in politics, medicine, law, religion, science, art, and, of course, the academy" (p. 13).

Science in particular is a masculine stronghold. It has been a "world without women" since the twelfth century. Here, Bleich (1990) draws on the work of David Noble, a historian who is studying the connections between the Roman Catholic Church and the academy. Women at one time "were relatively prominent in religious monasteries, often founding them" (Bleich, 1990, p. 232), but these monasteries gave way, around A.D. 1000, to all-male cathedral schools. (It was from these schools that the modern university evolved.) Subsequently, science and indeed all intellectual life in Catholic Europe were centered in the celibate church.[14]

The situation in Protestant England in the seventeenth century was not much different.

As Noble reminds us, Robert Boyle and Isaac Newton (from all the evidence available) never had female partners, and Boyle was given to practicing his science on Sunday, as a form of worship. Noble says similar attitudes about excluding women from science can be attributed to Galileo, Van Leeuwenhoek, and Gregor Mendel. In general, Noble thinks, most of the history of modern science shows that the exclusion of women and the hatred of women were defining elements of scientific culture and society. (Bleich, 1990, p. 232)

This is strong language, but evidence of science's "exclusion" and "hatred" of women has been presented by scholars such as Londa Schiebinger, Evelyn Fox Keller, Sandra Harding, and Laurel Furumoto. Schiebinger (1989, chap. 5) explains that in eighteenth-century France a "feminine" style of scholarship flourished briefly. In the aristocratic salons of Paris, knowledge was considered inseparable from refinement, gentility, politeness, and the eloquence with which it was expressed. Both men and women participated in this feminine style of intellectual activity, in contrast to the "pedantic" scholarship of the schools, which were all-male clubs. But critics of the salons, such as Jean Jacques Rousseau, argued that in the presence of women the "grave and serious" discourse of scholarship was diluted. The views of Rousseau prevailed: Because mental strength was seen to be correlated with physical strength, only men were considered capable of participating in the rigors of science.

Similarly, Keller (1982) argues that the emphasis in science on power and control, both of which are linked to aggression and "objectivity," is a projection of "a specifically male consciousness" (p. 598). That science had the power to subdue Nature—consistently portrayed as female—was clear enough in the writings of one of the fathers of modern science. Francis Bacon said that science is "leading to you Nature with all her children to bind her to your service and make her your slave"; science and the inventions it leads to do not "merely exert a gentle guidance over nature's course; they have the power to conquer and subdue her, to shake her to her foundations" (quoted by Keller, 1982, p. 598). Elsewhere, as Harding (1986) notes, Bacon explained the key features of the experimental method in terms suggestive of "men's most violent and misogynous relationships to women" (p. 116).

Masculine domination and exclusion of women is part of the history of psychology, as well. In a particularly telling example, Furumoto (1988) describes the Experimentalists, a society founded in 1904 by Edward

Titchener to promote his version of experimental psychology. The Experimentalists met each year at a different laboratory to discuss work in progress. One of the society's goals was to provide an informal setting where younger psychologists could meet and learn from more experienced ones. Women, however, were specifically excluded. The reason, according to one member, E. C. Sanford, was that "they [women] would undoubtedly interfere with the smoking and to a certain extent with the general freedom of a purely masculine assembly" (quoted by Furumoto, 1988, p. 104). As a result, Furumoto notes, female experimental psychologists were denied an important informal network of communication, and psychology was denied their contributions and point of view (pp. 94–95).[15]

Harding's (1986) argument, however, is not only that women have been excluded from psychological and other science (the "woman question" in science), but that science itself is so deeply patriarchal that a major transformation, along feminist lines, is in order (the "science question" in feminism).

In brief, the association between scientific practice and (masculine) aggression goes back to the beginnings of modern science, extends to the beginnings of modern psychology, and, according to many critics, is still much in evidence in science today. Bleich comments as follows:

Noble's historical perspective seems to make it clear that the practice of science (as we now know it) actually required the gathering of men together and, in a sense, "ganging up on" Nature, a female figure, to establish domination and control. What appears to be an epistemological approach—objectivity—is historically and culturally related to masculine domination of and violence toward women. (Bleich, 1990, p. 234)

ALTERNATIVE GENRES OF PSYCHOLOGICAL WRITING

My argument so far has been that the genres of academic discourse are permeated by competitiveness. In psychology, these ways of thinking and writing are so well learned that it's easy to overlook other possible ways of conducting the discipline's business. Recall Coe's (1987) argument that any genre motivates the search for particular types of information, thereby deflecting attention from other types. Alternative genres, therefore, can redirect our attention to kinds of psychological knowledge that otherwise would have been neglected. Work by composition specialists can help us remember and reclaim some other, "feminized" genres of academic writing.[16]

For example, the *exploratory essay* has been recommended by a number of composition scholars, including William Zeiger, Chris Anderson, and Joseph Comprone. Zeiger (1985) points out that "essay" comes from the French *essai*, to try or attempt. In this sense Michel de Montaigne's "Essaies" were trials or experiments, rather than definitive products. The kind of exploratory essay written by Montaigne contrasts with argumentative, persuasive, and informative essays that are concerned with upholding the truth of a proposition or demonstrating the validity of a thesis. In conventional academic writing, evidence is produced in support of a thesis, and, as we saw earlier in the work of Moulton, counterarguments are advanced to dispose of alternative explanations. But the exploratory essay is concerned not with demonstration, but with inquiry. It features a relatively "open" form, ambiguity, complexity, and nonlinear reasoning. In Zeiger's words, the exploratory essay "holds several possibilities in suspension simultaneously, inviting the inquisitive mind to play among them" (p. 457).[17]

Besides Montaigne, Zeiger mentions William Lamb, William Hazlitt, Annie Dillard, Joan Didion, and Garrison Keillor as skilled practitioners of the exploratory essay form. To this list, Anderson (1988) adds Samuel Johnson, Ralph Waldo Emerson, G. K. Chesterton, E. B. White, and Roland Barthes. Anderson agrees with Zeiger that the exploratory essay is associative and digressive in form. In this genre a writer doesn't have to pretend that everything is clear and worked out; uncertainty and ambiguity can be acknowledged.

Compared to the exclusionary nature of traditional academic and scientific discourse—the "we don't want to talk to you or hear from you unless you use our language" syndrome (Elbow, 1991, p. 147)—the exploratory essay is a relatively democratic genre. As Anderson points out, democratization was an important consideration for Emerson, who sought to liberate American culture from the "tyranny" of European professional scholarship. It was a question of access.

Access is also a feature mentioned by Comprone (1989), who studied the subgenre of *science essays*. Comprone was interested in how scientist-writers such as Stephen Jay Gould, Oliver Sacks, Lewis Thomas, and especially Loren Eiseley appeal to the layperson without compromising their science. He found that the texts of science essayists combine scientific vocabulary and reasoning with narration, description, and literary figures and schemes (see Chapter 4). Comprone (1989) speculates that these scientists, trying to make science comprehensible to the educated layperson, "have been driven by context and purpose to create hybrid or plural texts" (p. 113).[18] Whereas traditional scientific discourse tends to be exclusive, these alternative genres—blurred as they are—demystify.

Perhaps because of a concern to be seen as scientific, psychologists have generally shunned the exploratory essay and other alternative genres. One notable exception is Jerome Bruner, who is well known for his advocacy of narrative modes of thought alongside analytic ones (Bruner, 1986). In fact Bruner has been addressing the genre question for thirty years. In *On Knowing: Essays for the Left Hand*, Bruner (1962) makes much the same distinction between exploratory essays and demonstrative articles that Zeiger, Anderson, and Comprone made later, but Bruner does so using left/right imagery—the left hand being associated with intuition, dreams, and awkwardness; the right with order, lawfulness, and objectivity. By this metaphor, conventional psychological articles are right-handed. They "have about them an aseptic quality designed to proclaim the intellectual purity of our psychological enterprise," Bruner writes. "Perhaps this is well," he continues, "though it is not enough" (p. 5).

He grants that it is "economical" to report the products of research, rather than the "endless process" of research itself; yet something is missed when discourse is confined to the article (or empirical report) genre. Bruner is concerned

that we may be concealing some of the most fruitful sources of our ideas from one another. I have felt that the self-imposed fetish of objectivity has kept us from developing a needed genre of psychological writing—call it protopsychological writing if you will—the preparatory intellectual and emotional labors on which our later, more formalized, efforts are based. The genre in its very nature is literary and metaphoric, yet it is something more than this. It inhabits a realm midway between the humanities and the sciences. It is the left hand trying to transmit to the right. (Bruner, 1962, p. 5)

What Bruner calls the "self-imposed fetish of objectivity" may also be responsible for the tacit ban on personal experience. Even though, as Moulton (1983) observes, "experience may be a necessary element in certain reasoning processes" (p. 162), experience is usually not permitted to muddy the waters of pure philosophical—or psychological—discourse.

Bleich (1989) gives an example of how personal experience *can* be incorporated into academic writing; the result is perhaps a new, blurred genre. Ms. W, a folklore student, wrote an unusual paper for Bleich's graduate course in modern literary criticism. The first part of the paper was standard critical commentary on the short story, "Old Woman Magoun." Ms. W analyzed the structure of the story and made connections between it and Greek and Roman mythology. Then, switching from analytic to narrative mode, in the second part of the paper she discussed an episode from her own life that had parallels with the story. The second part of the paper showed why the story had such meaning for her, why she had chosen to work with it in the first place.

Ms. W's combining scholarly discourse and personal narrative raises questions about the appropriateness of mixing public argument and private experience (Tompkins, 1987). Certainly many academics would consider this to be unprofessional. As Elbow (1990) argues, however, there is nothing in the nature of personal expressive writing that is contrary to the aims of academic discourse: clear claims supported by reasons and evidence. Personal writing invites feeling but does not thereby exclude thinking. In short, writing that includes personal experience can do the work of academic discourse very well.

Besides including their *own* experience, psychologists can include the experience of research participants. Such vignettes contribute to psychological discourse because they can convey, as numbers cannot, the texture of experience. Piaget sometimes put his participants' words directly into his compositions. More recently, in works such as *In a Different Voice* (Gilligan, 1982) and *Women's Ways of Knowing* (Belenky, Clinchy, Goldberger, & Tarule, 1986), the words of the women interviewed are used extensively. Similarly, in *Feeding the Hungry Heart: The Experience of Compulsive Eating*, Geneen Roth (1983) includes both her own experience as an anorexic and, in their own words, the experiences of students in her program. In this way, as Chris Bullock (1990) observes, the reader of Roth's book can "come to identify with the voices closest to their own" (p. 145).

Summing up, what many of these examples have in common is a concern with *narrative*. The stories may be the writer's (as in the case of Ms. W), the participants' (as in *Women's Ways of Knowing*), or both (as in *Feeding the Hungry Heart*). Often different stories are interwoven. The effect then is one of multivocality or *heteroglossia* (Bakhtin, 1935/1981): Many voices are heard, rather than a single authoritative one.

A collection edited by Rhoda Unger (1989b) provides further evidence of psychology's narrative turn.[19] As Unger notes, many if not all the writers in *Representations: Social Constructions of Gender* are concerned with the telling of stories. When writing about gender, psychologists and others turn to narrative perhaps because it lends itself so well "to the exposition of different versions of consciousness. . . . It makes the fiction of one true reality harder to sustain" (Unger, 1989a, p. 3).

I would like to draw particular attention to two chapters in Unger's collection. As well as telling different types of stories, the chapters by

Michelle Fine and by M. Brinton Lykes suggest possibilities for reflexive modes of psychological writing.

Fine, a social psychologist, worked as a volunteer in rape counseling at a city hospital; her *Representations* chapter, written two years later, is in part a description of an encounter between herself and a female rape victim (Fine, 1989). As Fine presents it, the key issue is what it might mean for the victim to "take control." From a psychological—that is, individualistic—perspective, taking control means that the woman would draw on existing social institutions such as the justice system, taking legal action against the offender. What this perspective fails to notice, Fine argues, is that taking control may mean something quite different to people who are already the victims of racism and poverty and who are wary of the justice system. The rape victim that Fine talked with did not want to prosecute; she wanted to get home to her family, leaving justice in God's hands. Fine suggests that a feminist psychology needs to value this kind of "relational coping" and be willing to see victimization and control not from a distant social scientific standpoint, but contextually, through the eyes of the people affected.

To me the most interesting part of Fine's chapter is the final two pages, under the heading "Author's Note." Here, Fine does what one seldom sees in conventional empirical reports (Walsh-Bowers, 1992): She discusses her ambivalent feelings about the encounter and about publishing an account of it. The reasons for her ambivalence have to do with ethical issues of anonymity, informed consent, and the public use of information assumed at the time to be private. Although these issues aren't, and can't be, fully resolved, at least they are explicitly discussed. And out of this self-reflection come suggestions for others who may wish to use this research strategy intentionally and more systematically.

The chapter by Lykes is also concerned with the issue of control. Lykes's discussion of her own position in the research and of ethical and methodological issues is not confined to an author's note at the end, however; instead, the discussion continues throughout the entire article.

Lykes (1989) reports on her participatory research with Guatemalan Indian women living in exile. The chapter centers on issues of power and control in social science research, especially as these are embodied in the concept of informed consent. To put it simply, the research was going well—until Lykes introduced an informed consent form. The Guatemalan women saw no need to sign the form. As far as they were concerned, they had already given their consent when they agreed to tell their stories. Lykes's response was to try even harder to explain why the consent form was necessary.

I became increasingly invested in trying to clarify the form and why it was an important document that protected [their] interests. The traditionally trained social psychologist in me reacted almost mechanically and upon reflection I realize that *I* was shifting the context of our relationship, one that had been collaboratively constructed to that point. My own somewhat automatic response as social scientist took on a life of its own and prevented me from responding to the experience itself. (Lykes, 1989, p. 177)

What Lykes comes to realize is that the informed consent form—although seemingly straightforward and devised to protect the interests of the research participants—is actually a much more complex artifact, one with strong political and social overtones. The consent form releases the sponsoring institution from liability and gives the researcher the right to do with the data whatever she, as a scientist, deems appropriate. Thus it presupposes—and to some extent, creates—a power imbalance between researcher and participant; this causes a problem for activist research such as Lykes's, which aims at being collaborative and participatory. Lykes introduced the consent form to protect her participants, but found that she had created a barrier instead: "I was, on the one hand, seeking to protect myself while, on the other hand, implicitly asserting that I needed to protect them from abuses of my control" (Lykes, 1989, p. 178).

In Unger's book, then, and especially perhaps in the chapters by Fine and Lykes, we can glimpse some new or renewed genres of psychological writing. Unger's writers are able to find ways of writing that allow them to tell stories, include their own experience, and reflect on the ethics, limitations, and ambiguities of their research, all of which are difficult or impossible to do within the genre of the empirical report as currently sanctioned. These alternative kinds of discourse are examples of what I am calling a "feminized" writing of psychology.

CONCLUSION

One needn't be a feminist, of course, to write outside the traditional genres. We saw earlier that psychologists as diverse as Bruner, Nisbett, McConnell, and Skinner have all turned to alternative genres on occasion. We considered, too, a radical experiment in psychological writing—George Howard's *Tale of Two Stories* (1989)—in which chapters of personal narrative alternate with history of science. In her review, Jill Morawski (1990) agrees that the book's unique feature is its form. But she is pointedly noncommittal on whether this kind of writing is appropriate in academic psychology.

As part autobiography, part informal and stylistic history of science, and part chatty dialogue, the text left this reviewer with some sticky questions: What is accomplished by departing from the conventions of scientific writing? What is compromised by such a departure? Why autobiography? . . . Each reader should use *A Tale of Two Stories* to consider the limitations of, and possibilities for, new genres of reflexive writing in the human sciences. (Morawski, 1990, pp. 465–466)

Morawski's ambivalence suggests that "the conventions of scientific writing" are strong indeed. In order to understand what these conventions are and where their strength comes from, it is necessary to consider in greater detail the dominant genre in psychology: the empirical report. As we will see in Chapter 4, psychologists have long been taught to write in a certain highly prescribed style. Composition scholars, though, can teach us to question it.

Chapter Four

The Elements of APA Style

Again and again, language has been considered to be a problem, a phenomenon that obscures true knowledge.
                                        —Karen Burke LeFevre (1987, p. 99)

I had always thought "Strunk and White" deserved to be the most popular stylebook ever written. First published in 1959, the book has helped several generations of writers achieve a sharper, more concise style. Based on my experience with *The Elements of Style* (Strunk & White, 1979), I had to agree with the writers of the *Publication Manual of the American Psychological Association* (1983) who describe it as "a classic that offers concise, clear advice on writing well" (p. 184).

I was surprised, then, when I learned that in composition studies *The Elements of Style* is not universally admired. Richard Ohmann (1979), for instance, is critical of Strunk and White's advice to "use definite, specific, concrete language."

Does anyone besides me feel uneasy when Strunk and White begin exemplifying this reasonable advice? For "A period of unfavorable weather set in," they substitute "It rained every day for a week." The rewrite is indeed more definite, specific, and concrete, and less pompous to boot. But it doesn't say the same thing, and in that difference there is a loss as well as a gain, especially if the writer means to relate the weather to some undertaking rather than just describing it. The original conveys—however inadequately—a more complex idea. The same is true when "He showed satisfaction as he took possession of his well-earned

reward" becomes for Strunk and White "He grinned as he pocketed the coin."
(Ohmann, 1979, p. 390)

Ohmann considers examples of writing from three other composition
handbooks in addition to *The Elements of Style*; a *handbook* may be
defined as "a compendium of rules, models, and exercises covering
aspects of formal and syntactic convention" (Connors, 1983b, p. 87). In
each example considered, the version that the handbook prefers is, in
Ohmann's view, poorer—less complex, less thoughtful—than the version
it doesn't prefer. The problem with using definite, specific, and concrete
language is that it keeps writers on the surfaces of things—as if their only
goal were to transmit immediate information. According to Ohmann, the
handbooks direct attention to everyday things and thereby deflect attention
from more considered, abstract inquiry into the historical, social, and
political relevance of those things.[1]

From my point of view, one of the values of Ohmann's essay is that it
reminds us that texts—even classics such as Strunk and White's—are
never beyond criticism. By giving voice to some of the unstated assumptions of composition handbooks, Ohmann shows how other disciplines
might similarly reexamine their classic texts.

What are the equivalent documents in our discourse community? Although psychology may not have handbooks in the strict sense of the term,
the APA *Publication Manual* fits at least two-thirds of the definition: It is
indeed a "compendium" of "rules" and "models" (although not exercises)[2]
"covering aspects of formal and syntactic convention." Because it emphasizes form and mechanical correctness, the *Manual* could be further
specified as a "current-traditional" handbook.[3]

Like many composition handbooks, especially current-traditional ones,
the *Manual* presents itself as ideologically neutral; it does not announce
any particular theoretical or philosophical position. But its neutrality
should at least be questioned. The *Manual* is, after all, one of psychology's
premier "charter documents" (McCarthy, 1991): On the one hand, it
reflects, however imperfectly, the discipline's current consensus about
standards and conventions of written psychology; on the other, it serves
to project those standards and conventions onto new generations of
psychology writers. Lucille McCarthy explains the significance of charter
documents:

The charter document of a social or political group establishes an organizing
framework that specifies what is significant and draws people's attention to
certain rules and relationships. In other words, the charter defines as authoritative

certain ways of seeing and deflects attention from other ways. It thus stabilizes a particular reality and sets the terms for future discussions. (McCarthy, 1991, p. 359)

McCarthy's own work focuses on psychiatry. She presents a case study of a biomedically oriented psychiatrist using the third edition of the *Diagnostic and Statistical Manual of Mental Disorders (DSM-III-R*; American Psychiatric Association, 1987). As a charter document in psychiatry, the *DSM-III-R* shapes and stabilizes reality for this psychiatrist; it informs what she knows about mental illness and how she writes about it.

Similarly, I suggest, the APA *Publication Manual* "stabilizes a particular reality" for psychologists. It defines as authoritative certain ways of seeing, certain ways of doing and writing psychology, and thereby deflects attention from other ways of seeing, doing, and writing. In other words, the explicit and implicit rules embodied in the *Manual* have an epistemological function: By determining how we can write, the rules shape what we can know. In this sense, APA style stabilizes reality for the discipline as a whole.

In suggesting that the *Manual* is a significant document, I am not suggesting that all psychologists have learned it by heart. Undoubtedly there are many who do not own it, have never read it, or consult it only rarely. Nevertheless, we are all influenced by "APA style." That influence is seen, for instance, in the uniform compositional style of research reports published between 1939 and 1989 (Walsh-Bowers, 1992). As Richard Walsh-Bowers (1992) shows, the laboratory rhetoric favored by the *Manual*—use of the term *subjects*, for example—extends even to interpersonal subdisciplines such as educational psychology, where it would seem to be inappropriate. The dictates of APA style extend well beyond the covers of the *Manual*; they are reproduced in countless handbooks, guides, and research design textbooks, both in psychology and even generally in the social sciences. Even the rival American Psychological Society has adopted the APA code.

APA style is much more than a particular citation system, therefore. I would like to use the broad heading of *style* to consider the kinds of writing and knowing the *Manual* makes available and unavailable. Following Ohmann's lead, I will try to make some of the *Manual*'s unstated assumptions explicit; along the way, I will sketch in the historical background so we can see where these assumptions come from.

In this chapter I will follow my usual strategy of discussing psychology—in this case, the APA *Manual*—from the perspective of composition studies. Specifically, my treatment owes a great deal to the work of the composition specialist Charles Bazerman (1988). I will refer throughout to Bazerman's chapter "Codifying the Social Scientific Style: The APA *Publication Manual* as a Behaviorist Rhetoric," especially since that essay is not as widely known in psychology as it should be.

PRELIMINARY CONSIDERATIONS

Prescriptivism

A stylesheet for psychology first appeared in 1929 as a 6.5-page article in the *Psychological Bulletin* (Bentley et al., 1929). In 1944, John Anderson and Willard Valentine published a thirty-two page paper on the preparation of articles for APA journals. The first official edition of the *Publication Manual* was published in 1952 (sixty-one pages), revised in 1957 and again in 1967. The second edition appeared in 1974 (136 pages), and the third in 1983 (208 pages).

Thus the most obvious historical trend is the increasing length of the *Manual*. And, as Bazerman observes, with increased length has come increased prescriptiveness. The committee responsible for the original stylesheet in 1929 declined to assume any authority over authors, publishers, or editors; it merely offered a set of "recommendations." By 1983 this gentle tone had disappeared. The *Manual* is now unashamedly prescriptive; its purpose is to provide "rules" (p. 11).

A prescriptive approach makes complex, situation-dependent notions into universal standards for all writing. Whereas composition specialists tend to see writing as shaped by the variable nature of writers' purposes, readers, and the occasions that call forth the writing, the *Manual* seems to suggest that these are all fixed entities. With purpose, readers, and occasion stabilized, writing can now be presented as a matter of following rules.[4]

And rules are what the *Manual* provides. Thus, for example, the rule for verbs is to "use the active rather than the passive voice" (p. 36), and is illustrated by the following pair of sentences:

Poor: The experiment was designed by Gould (1970).

Better: Gould (1970) designed the experiment. (American Psychological Association, 1983, p. 36)

But, as Ohmann might point out, the two sentences don't say the same thing. The first is a statement about the experiment; the second a statement about Gould. On what basis, then, could one be "better" than the other? Wouldn't it be more accurate and helpful to say that which one is more effective in a given situation depends, among other things, on what the writer is trying to say?

Introduction-Method-Results-and-Discussion Form

Related to the *Manual*'s increasing prescriptiveness is its increasingly hard-line position on the *form* of the psychology article. In the early years of modern psychology, writers of empirical reports used whatever sections seemed appropriate; the earliest stylesheets favored ad-hoc headings. "Necessary headings only should be inserted," the Committee on Form of Manuscript wrote in 1929 (Bentley et al., p. 58), and Anderson and Valentine (1944) called for "appropriate headings" (p. 351). But by the mid-1950s most empirical writing in science, including psychology, was using the now familiar four-section format: introduction-method-results-and-discussion—or IMRAD, for short. It wasn't until the second edition (American Psychological Association, 1974), however, that the *Manual* unequivocally endorsed the IMRAD format. In summary, whereas writers of empirical reports in psychology originally used whatever headings were most appropriate to their projects, writers today are almost invariably required to use IMRAD form.[5]

As well as specifying more and more precisely what sections should be used, later versions of the *Manual* are increasingly explicit about what each should contain. Whereas the first edition (American Psychological Association Council of Editors, 1952) devotes less than one page to content, the third edition (American Psychological Association, 1983) has about six times as much (pp. 22–29). Psychology writers today are told what sections to use and what to say in each one.

The notion of fixed sections with fixed content is not a recent one, however. Historians of rhetoric trace the origins of this idea to the French scholar Peter Ramus (1515–1572). Ramus challenged the classical idea, originating with Aristotle, that the domain of *rhetoric* encompassed the five elements of invention, arrangement, style, memory, and delivery. Ramus reallocated invention and arrangement to *logic*, leaving only style and delivery under rhetoric. (He ignored memory.) In effect, Ramus drove a wedge between logic and rhetoric, thus contributing to a long-lasting split between "reason" and "imagination" (Corbett, 1990, p. 556).

Ramus's maneuver has two important consequences for psychology. First, the redefinition of "invention" as a matter of logic, rather than rhetoric, makes it more possible for the discipline to determine content, to decide what needs to be said. Now individual writers do not have to think about what should be mentioned in a particular section because this has already been collectively predetermined, on logical grounds. Second, if "arrangement"—deciding what goes where—is also seen as a matter of logic, it means that, once a particular arrangement has been identified as the logical one, responsibility for determining order is also effectively out of writers' hands.

Thus, when writers of psychology are told to use fixed sections with fixed content in a fixed order, the clear implication is that these are logical and not rhetorical concerns.[6] Logic and *chrono*logic appear to be the basis of the *Manual*'s statement that empirical reports "typically consist of [four] distinct sections that *reflect the stages in the research process and that appear in the sequence of these stages*" (1983, p. 21, emphasis added). But the assumptions underlying this statement can be challenged. Is there just one research process? Does it have stages? Are there exactly four? Do they always occur in the same order? The *Manual* presents one model of research as if it were the only one.

When information appears in a fixed place, both writing and reading become more efficient. On the other hand, there are several drawbacks. As pointed out by Bazerman (1988), scientist-writers are now less likely to stop and think about the significance of the information they are presenting, "whether it and other possible information should be included, and exactly how this information should be placed in the structure of the whole article" (p. 260).

Researchers using the IMRAD format also needn't establish continuity between the parts of the article. Scientists know that methods and results, for example, are connected: A particular method is chosen for its potential to yield a certain type of result, and certain results are rejected because of the methods used to obtain them (Knorr-Cetina, 1981, p. 122). Nevertheless, in the IMRAD structure, "method" and "results" are separate entities. Writers do not have to show how they are conceptually related; nor, indeed, do they have to demonstrate the coherence of the entire enterprise (Bazerman, 1988, p. 260).

The ultimate problem with prescriptivism and rigid formats, however, is that they disempower, or "deauthorize," writers. In fact there is little room in the *Publication Manual* for writers or writing. Instead, it "convey[s] the impression that writing is primarily a matter of applying established rules" (Bazerman, 1988, p. 259). Sometimes this is considered an advantage; it does, after all, seem to simplify the writer's task. Daryl Bem (1987), for instance, says that "the first step toward clarity is good organization, and the standardized format of a journal article does much of the work for you" (p. 173). To a critic like Bazerman, though, having a standardized format do the work instead of the writer is not necessarily a positive development.

Incremental Encyclopedism

In his historical survey, Bazerman shows that, as empirical psychology developed, *methods* gradually became less important and *results* more so. In the early years of modern psychology (ca. 1880–1915), authors spent considerable time explaining their methods, showing how they were appropriate to the (philosophical) problem at hand. But by the 1930s or so, methods had become less interesting. Now they were more a demonstration of carefulness and competence than an exercise in good reasoning; their main function, Bazerman (1988) suggests, was "to protect the researcher's results by showing that the experiment was done cleanly and correctly" (p. 272). In 1932, the *Journal of Experimental Psychology* began publishing methods sections in reduced type—a clear sign of their reduced status. (To this day, APA journals print methods in smaller type.)

As methods became less prominent rhetorically and visually, the results section took up the slack. In Bazerman's (1988) argument, it was the growing influence of behaviorism that caused results to be increasingly presented not as answers to theoretical questions, but as "ends in themselves, to fill out gaps in other results" (p. 273). The tendency to make results the center of the empirical report—its point, or news—implies a philosophy of science that Bazerman calls *incremental encyclopedism* (p. 273). Each article is seen to contribute another fact to the cumulative storehouse of scientific knowledge.

This encyclopedic view of science contrasts sharply, of course, with the view presented in Chapter 2. We saw there that one advantage of abandoning the audience metaphor is that it enables a more dynamic, interactive conception of science. In this perspective, knowledge is not deposited in storehouses, but constructed through the ongoing conversations of particular discourse communities.[7]

Bazerman makes the point that the author–date citation system—a standard feature of APA style since 1967—makes it even more likely that articles will be treated as self-contained entities. By putting forward author–date associations as items for conscious attention, this system enables them to "serve as kinds of facts in the argument" (Bazerman, 1988, p. 263). He might have added that the author–date system often results in disruptive competence displays—citation bingeing—as writers seemingly attempt to impress readers with the breadth of their knowledge. Furthermore, it tends to foreground timeliness, "Smith, 1993" being a more persuasive citation than "Smith, 1963."[8]

Nevertheless, the philosophy of incremental encyclopedism is expressed not only in a particular citation system. The *Manual* consistently imagines science as an accumulation of knowledge bits. Thus, for example, the scientific journal is "the repository of the accumulated knowledge of a field," investigators "build on existing work," and high-quality journal articles contribute to a field's "growth" (American Psychological Association, 1983, p. 17). What is interesting here are the metaphors of building and growing—clear evidence, I think, of incrementalism. Just as interesting is the *Manual*'s identification of the scientific journal as a repository. Webster's *New World Dictionary* of 1966 lists six meanings of "repository," of which the fifth, "anything thought of as a place of accumulation or storage," is no doubt the intended one. What troubles me, however, are some of repository's other senses: "a box, chest, closet, or room in which things may be placed for safekeeping," or, even more ominously, "a burial vault; a sepulcher."

PLAIN STYLE

Over time, as Bazerman suggests, psychological style has become more rigid in form and more strongly committed to incremental encyclopedism. But composition scholars can also help us examine style at a finer level of analysis. To do that, we will need to turn to the current (third) edition of the *Manual*[9] and compare its prescriptions with work from composition studies.

What is the style recommended for psychologists? The *Manual* says, "simplicity, plain language, and direct statements will always suffice" (p. 14). Let us give the name of *plain style* to that which will always suffice, and consider three aspects of plain style that are especially prominent in the *Manual*: clarity, literal writing, and brevity.

Clarity

Clarity may be the key word in the *Manual*—its "god term" (Weaver, 1953). "Write in clear and vigorous prose" (p. 24). "Thoughtful concern for the language can yield clear and orderly writing" (p. 31). "Clear communication . . . is the prime objective of scientific writing" (p. 31). And so on. In the first twenty-eight pages of the *Manual*, "clear" and "clarity" are used twenty-two times.

Clarity is associated with other virtues:

Clear communication . . . may be achieved by presenting ideas in an orderly manner and by expressing oneself smoothly and precisely. By developing ideas clearly and logically, you invite readers to read, encourage them to continue, and make their task agreeable by leading them smoothly from thought to thought. (American Psychological Association, 1983, p. 31)

Thus "clear," "smooth," and "logical" writing go together; in fact, the terms are virtually interchangeable. Scientific writing that is clear, smooth, and logical is, in a word, *good*.

Literal Writing

At the same time that psychology writers are urged toward clarity, we are warned against literary or "creative" writing. In the *Manual*, scientific and creative writing are presented as sharply separated types. Whereas scientific writing at its best is invisible, creative writing draws attention to itself with metaphors, similes, and other "poetic expressions."

Although scientific and literary writing may indeed have different purposes and occasions, what I am drawing attention to is the black-and-white picture painted by the *Manual*. In Chapter 3 we considered Ralph Cohen's argument that genres are both "necessary" and "loose"; in the *Manual*, however, they are only necessary. No room here for Geertz's (1983) blurred genres.

Furthermore, although at times the *Manual* presents the issue in terms of what is "appropriate" for different kinds of writing, at other times it appears to be making a value judgment, with scientific writing portrayed as the better kind. Thus literary devices are to be avoided because they "can *confuse* or *disturb* readers of scientific prose" (p. 32, emphasis added). And, in a revealing word choice, the writers of the *Manual* say that "unconstrained wordiness lapses into embellishment and literary elegance" (p. 34). Why "lapses"?

The *Manual* provides a list of literary figures that writers of psychology should avoid.

Devices that attract attention to words, sounds, or other embellishments instead of to ideas are inappropriate in scientific writing. Avoid heavy alliteration, accidental rhyming, poetic expressions, and clichés. Use metaphors sparingly; although they can help simplify complicated ideas, metaphors can be distracting. (American Psychological Association, 1983, p. 43)

Brevity

Finally, the *Manual* values brevity. "Say only what needs to be said," writers are advised (p. 33).[10] Although hardly a model of conciseness itself, the *Manual* goes on to give some ways of achieving it:

You can tighten overly long papers by eliminating redundancy, wordiness, jargon, evasiveness, circumlocution, and clumsiness. Weed out overly detailed descriptions of apparatus, subjects, or procedure; gratuitous embellishments; elaborations of the obvious; and irrelevant observations or asides. (American Psychological Association, 1983, p. 33)

Another way to achieve brevity is to avoid discursive or content footnotes, defined as those that "supplement or amplify substantive information in the text" (p. 105). Such notes are discouraged, on the grounds that they are expensive to print and "distracting to readers."

So these three—clarity, literal writing, and brevity—are significant aspects of the plain style prescribed in the current edition of the APA *Manual*. There is, however, a long tradition of plain style in scientific writing. If we examine that tradition it will help us understand current practices.

A BRIEF HISTORY OF PLAIN STYLE

Plain style in the modern sense can be traced to the Royal Society in seventeenth-century England; but long before that, authorities had something to say about clarity, literal writing, and brevity. In Book III of his *Rhetoric*, Aristotle emphasized clarity as one of the most important aspects of style. However, he also said, "Nobody uses fine language when teaching geometry" (quoted by Halloran & Bradford, 1984, p. 180)—the implication being that different styles are appropriate for different speaking situations, whether deliberative, forensic, or ceremonial (Halloran & Whitburn, 1982, p. 61).

More complex than Aristotle's was the treatment of style developed by Cicero (106–43 B.C.). As S. Michael Halloran and Merrill Whitburn (1982) explain, for Cicero, plain style was one of three levels, the others being middle and grand style. Plain style was closest to actual speech. Metaphors were encouraged because they were common in speech. Whereas Aristotle associated different styles with different speaking situations, Cicero associated styles with the effects a speaker intended to bring about in an audience: plain style was for instructing, middle style for pleasing, and grand style for moving to action and belief. In practice, however, orators were encouraged to mix all three styles in the same speech. Instruction, delight, and persuasion were inseparable. The three rhetorical functions, and therefore the three styles, were aspects of "the single process of communication by which one human intelligence influences another" (Halloran & Whitburn, 1982, p. 62).

Although Cicero's work did much to mediate the dispute between the Asiatics, who favored a florid, highly mannered style, and the Atticists, who favored a plain, severe style (Corbett, 1990, p. 546)—and although Cicero recommended that orators integrate all three levels—by the time of the Renaissance, Cicero's name was linked to a florid, "abundant" style of speaking and writing. Abundance was the topic of a treatise by Erasmus (ca. 1466–1536), the most influential rhetorician of the Renaissance (Corbett, 1990, p. 550). In his 1512 book *De Copia*, Erasmus showed how to expand a discourse in a controlled way. As Edward Corbett (1990, p. 551) observes, fullness of expression was partly a matter of invention (saying more things about a given topic) and partly a matter of style (saying one thing in more ways). To illustrate the latter, stylistic variation, Erasmus gives 141 ways of saying "Your letter pleased me mightily" and no fewer than 200 variations of "Always, as long as I live, I shall remember you" (Erasmus, 1512/1978, pp. 348–364). For instance:

- Never, as long as I live, shall I fail to remember you.

- As long as I have breath, I shall be found mindful of you.

- I shall begin to forget myself before I begin to forget you. (Erasmus, 1512/1978, p. 355)[11]

A practical application of abundant style was the art of preaching. The biblical injunction to "increase and multiply" was given rhetorical meaning as preachers of the day sought to divide, open up, and expatiate on a closed or difficult scriptural text. John Donne wrote, "Through partition or division, the Word of God is made a Sermon, that is, a Text is dilated, diffused into a Sermon" (quoted by Parker, 1987, p. 14).

Meanwhile, Renaissance religious leaders considered science to be little better than witchcraft. As Galileo learned, scientists had to make their pronouncements consistent with church doctrine or be branded heretical. The result for scientific writing, as Halloran and Annette Bradford (1984) point out, was that emerging scientific theories (such as Johannes Kepler's) were expressed in language "bordering on the mystical"—

convoluted enough to confuse the superstitious yet comprehensible enough to transmit ideas to other members of the scientific community. Renaissance scientific style, then, was a confusing verbal smoke screen, a cloak of mystical gibberish with the antithetical goals of expression and obscurity. (Halloran & Bradford, 1984, p. 181)

This was the background against which modern science emerged in the seventeenth century. Considering the ornamental excesses and deliberate obscurities of the Renaissance, it is understandable that the new scientists would react by advocating plain style.

Francis Bacon, for example, complained that in Renaissance discourse the emphasis was improperly on words, choice phrases, figures, and tropes; what *should* be of concern, he said, was "weight of matter, worth of subject, soundness of argument" (quoted by Corbett, 1990, p. 559). For the writing of natural and experimental history, at least, Bacon advocated a plain, utilitarian style—writing shorn of all "ornaments of speech, similitudes, treasury of eloquence, and such like emptinesses" in favor of "things . . . set down briefly and concisely, so that they may be nothing less than words" (quoted by Zappen, 1989, p. 82).[12]

Like Bacon, Thomas Sprat was suspicious of "literary" language, asking "how many mists and uncertainties, these specious *Tropes* and *Figures* have brought on our Knowledg?" (1667/1959, p. 112). In the name of brevity Sprat urged fellow members of the Royal Society "to reject all the amplifications, digressions, and swellings of style: to return back to the primitive purity, and shortness, when men deliver'd so many *things*, almost in an equal number of *words*" (p. 113).[13]

Sprat suggested that members of the Royal Society strive for *clarity*—

a close, naked, natural way of speaking; positive expressions; clear senses; a native easiness: bringing all things as near the Mathematical plainness, as they can: and preferring the language of Artizans, Countrymen, and Merchants, before that, of Wits, or Scholars. (Sprat, 1667/1959, p. 113)

About seventeenth-century plain style there is good news and bad. As suggested by Sprat's reference to "Artizans, Countrymen, and Merchants," plain style made room for wider participation in science than had been the case previously. For Bacon, too, plain style was a political issue insofar as a democratic science could involve everyone—or at least every *man* (Zappen, 1989, p. 83). The bad news is that the privileging of "Mathematical plainness" and the sharp separation of the senses, reason, and imagination contributed to a positivist approach to both science and language that has dominated scientific writing ever since.

Plain Style in Psychology

Fast forward now to the late nineteenth century and the emergence of modern psychology. As we have seen, an official stylesheet for psychologists did not appear until 1929. Before then, individuals and journal editors were free to make whatever pronouncements they liked.

G. Stanley Hall was apparently the first editor to make such a statement, and he spoke up for brevity. Reacting against both the "armchair professors" of the United States as well as "prominent German experimenters," Hall (1895) announced that the *American Journal of Psychology* would give preference to reports of psychophysics experiments, "provided, always, that there is the greatest practicable condensation and elimination of excessive discussion and unimportant details" (p. 5).

Brevity continued to be a highly valued property of psychological writing throughout the twentieth century. The committee responsible for the 1929 stylesheet urged writers "to be as brief as possible without sacrificing clarity or pertinent facts" (Bentley et al., p. 57). "Short sentences and short paragraphs should be employed wherever feasible," they added (p. 58). The first edition of the *Publication Manual* (American Psychological Association Council of Editors, 1952) warned against "discursive writing" and advised writers to "try rewriting each paragraph in reduced length, but with the same substance" (pp. 10–11).

Clarity was also highly prized. The 1929 stylesheet recommended that the discussion section of an experimental article be "clear and straightforward" (Bentley et al., p. 59). In the 1944 version, Anderson and Valentine said that "clarity of expression" is essential in a satisfactory manuscript (p. 347).

Thus brevity and clarity have long been associated with good writing in psychology. Warnings against so-called literary language, however, have been made only recently. Until the second edition of the *Manual* (American Psychological Association, 1974), there was virtually no official criticism of the judicious use of imaginative language. On the contrary, in 1944 Anderson and Valentine endorsed the use of "schemes"—variations or embellishments of standard syntax.

Particular care should be taken to avoid the constant use of simple declarative sentences of uniform length, or of a series of citations which always begin with the author's name. This habit makes for a heavy and monotonous style that is devoid of interest. By varying sentence length and structure, by employing well-chosen subordinate phrases and clauses, and by the use of vigorous and apt expression, authors help their readers and increase the effect of their articles.

Authors are also urged to give articles a final and careful literary revision with a view to improving style. (Anderson & Valentine, 1944, p. 350)

Later editions of the *Manual* continue to endorse schemes but are skeptical of other devices. The second edition explains that "heavy alliteration, accidental rhymes, poetic expressions, and clichés" are to be avoided because "they lead the reader, who is looking for information, away from the theme of the paper" (American Psychological Association, 1974, p. 28).[14] In the third edition, literary devices that attract attention to "words, sounds, or other embellishments"—rather than to "ideas"—are said to be "inappropriate" (American Psychological Association, 1983, p. 43).

PLAIN STYLE RECONSIDERED

In psychology, it has long been taken as self-evident that scientific writing is different from creative writing, and that psychologists, because they are not poets, should strive to be plain, clear, and concise. Plain style has been the norm in science ever since the seventeenth century, but, as the preceding historical overview shows, it arose in the first place as a reaction against the ornamental excesses of the Renaissance. Is some sort of middle ground possible? I believe it is; but in order to understand why it is necessary, we need first to understand in greater depth what is entailed by *clarity*, *literal writing*, and *brevity*. In the following sections, work by composition scholars will be used to help us critically examine these notions.

Clarity

It goes without saying that it is a good thing to be "clear." On the other hand, anything that goes without saying should by that very fact make us suspicious: Whose desire is it that we not examine and speak about clarity? What, after all, is at stake in linguistic clarity? At the outset it should be recognized that "clarity" is a metaphor, and that—like the metaphor of "audience" (Chapter 2)—it may carry baggage we don't necessarily want.

The metaphor of clear language suggests that we should be able to look right through it and see something else on the other side. And what we see, apparently, is the author's ideas. To use the metaphor of clarity, then, is to think of language as a window through which a reader perceives a writer's meaning. In a classic description of the windowpane theory of language, James Sutherland (1957) writes, "It is good prose when it allows the writer's meaning to come through with the least possible loss of significance and nuance, as a landscape is seen through a clear window" (p. 77). The suggestion is that the best texts are the least visible—the "cleanest windows."[15]

Carolyn Miller (1979) explores some implications of windowpane theory for scientific and technical writing. Miller alludes to the positivist tradition in science, in which knowledge "is a matter of getting closer to the material things of reality and farther away from the confusing and untrustworthy imperfections of words and minds" (p. 610). In this tradition the role of language is, again, to act as a window through which the real world can be apprehended. Clear language allows readers to see reality accurately; opaque or decorative language makes them see what is not really there or forces them to see it only with difficulty.

In the positivist tradition, knowledge is a commodity and the purpose of writing is to transmit this commodity from author to reader (Reddy, 1979). Rhetoric is seen as irrelevant to this purpose. Indeed the rhetoric of positivism is an "anti-rhetoric rhetoric"—rhetoric that denies being a rhetoric—and "technical and scientific writing become just a series of maneuvers for staying out of the way" (C. Miller, 1979, p. 613).[16]

I wish to draw attention to Miller's claim that positivist science considers language "confusing and untrustworthy," because these terms—suggesting as they do a moral dimension—seem to account for many of the APA *Manual*'s prescriptions. Indeed the *Manual* preaches a kind of Puritan ethic. Scientific language ought to be plain, frugal, and unadorned; if we start dressing it up with embellishments, we will distract the reader from the real work we're trying to do. No ornaments please, we're scientists.[17]

Clarity thus has positivist and moralist dimensions. Moreover, talking about clarity as if it were a simple property of texts obscures one obvious yet crucial fact: What is clear to you might not be clear to me. And what is clear on one occasion might not be on another. Thus clarity should be considered not a stable property of texts, but a relationship or set of relationships among writer, reader, text, and situation. It is a more complex concept than usually made out to be. Knowledge, familiarity, and expectations play important roles in determining what is clear on any given occasion for any given reader. Richard Lanham writes:

Clarity (as central normative standard for "good prose") does more harm than good. For clarity is not any single verbal configuration but a relationship between writer and reader. There are all kinds of clarities. . . . When you say that a prose is clear, you are rewarding success, but the success may be of many kinds, the rewarding for many reasons. Thus the injunction "Be clear!" really amounts to

"Succeed!", "Write good prose!", or in cant, "Communicate!" Such advice is bracing but not very helpful. (Lanham, 1974, p. 32)

Similarly, the *Manual*'s injunction "Be clear!" amounts to "Write like a psychologist!" Bracing, but not very helpful.

I should emphasize that my purpose here is not to advocate obscurity, but to examine what is implicit in the notion of clarity. I would conclude by agreeing that clarity is indeed a fine thing—but then, so is effectiveness and so is success. Since clarity means so many different things in different situations, the all-purpose advice to "be clear," although well meaning, is quite empty.

Literal Writing

In 1667 Thomas Sprat (1667/1959) warned against the "trick" of metaphors in scientific writing. More than three centuries later the APA *Manual* discourages psychologists from using metaphors because they "can be distracting" (p. 43). Apparently, it is the writer's ideas that readers can be distracted from—in this windowpane philosophy, a sharp distinction is made between *ideas* (thought, meaning) and their *expression* (language). It is also assumed that ideas occur *before* language: Writers "have" ideas, then clothe them in revealing, see-through words. The idea/expression dichotomy recalls other, similar distinctions between logic and rhetoric (Ramus), reason and imagination (Bacon). But can thought and language be so neatly separated?

Evidently not—for, even as psychology officially discourages figurative language, it relies on it. As Halloran and Bradford (1984) note, "For all it protests to the contrary, science has and does rely on the power of [literary] figures" (p. 183). After all, science is more than careful observation: Whenever an analogy is proposed, a synthesis achieved, a model postulated, or a paradigm established, scientists are taking metaphoric leaps into "a realm of thought outside the literal world" (p. 183). Psychologists could not do psychology without nonliteral thought and language.

Halloran and Bradford use the concept of DNA to illustrate the pervasiveness of metaphor in science. The standard model of DNA as communication is itself a metaphor: DNA is portrayed as a code that transmits genetic messages. Even in specialist journals of molecular biology, Halloran and Bradford found that metaphoric terms are used to describe the complexities of DNA—terms like "expression," "translation," "messenger," "comma-free code," "editing," and "reading" (p. 186). If *basic metaphors* are the powerful, usually unarticulated schemas that we live and work by (Lakoff & Johnson, 1980), DNA as communication is such a metaphor: It organizes scientists' experience and sets their research agendas.

Halloran and Bradford (1984) make a distinction between basic metaphors and *local metaphors*. The latter serve a short-term communication function but don't organize experience, at least not over the long term (pp. 187–188). For example, the DNA molecule has been likened to a spiral staircase and a zipper. Nevertheless, it would be a mistake, I think, to make local and basic into absolute categories; this would be yet another instance of thought/expression dualism. The main point is that metaphors are figures of thought *and* language (Lakoff, 1986).

Metaphors and other figures are pervasive in the natural and social sciences (Hoffman, 1980). Even the writers of the *Manual* were unable to resist advising psychologists to "weed out" superfluous language (p. 33); elsewhere they say that components of long sentences should "march along like people in a parade, not dodge about like broken-field runners" (p. 34). The most extensive discussion of metaphors in psychology, however, is in the collection edited by David Leary (1990). The essays in his *Metaphors in the History of Psychology* leave little doubt that metaphors—both local and basic—have played and continue to play an important role in psychological thought and writing.

To note just a few examples: "Memory" has historically been considered a wax tablet, a dictionary, an encyclopedia, a muscle, a telephone switchboard, a computer, a hologram (Hoffman, Cochran, & Nead, 1990, p. 182); "consciousness" has been likened to a spotlight, a footlight, a flowing river, a stream of thoughts, a seamless web, a graph, a powerless rider, a recursive loop, a readout, a pandemonium, a stage (Bruner & Feldman, 1990, p. 230); in motivational accounts, "people" have been considered pawns, agents, natural entities, organisms, and machines (McReynolds, 1990, p. 139). Metaphor can be found even where we might not have expected it—in the work of neobehaviorists such as Edward C. Tolman, Clark Hull, and B. F. Skinner (Smith, 1990). (For example, consider Skinner's metaphoric concepts of shaping, extinction, and superstitious behaviors; Smith, 1990, pp. 255–256.)

So, no matter how much the official stylesheets warn against the dangers of metaphor and other literary embellishments, psychologists have never been able to live without them. One reason may be that metaphors are helpful—if not absolutely essential—for the development of theory. Metaphors link two domains. The metaphor *mind is energy*, for example, associates the mind with an energy system, yet it leaves open which particular aspect of the system is emphasized. As Kurt Danziger (1990b) suggests, theorists create different theoretical accounts by emphasizing different aspects. Alexander Bain and William McDougall both conceived the mind as an energy system: Bain was interested in the problem of harnessing mental energy, whereas McDougall was interested in how a continued supply of energy was guaranteed. Metaphors thus not only provide a framework for shared discourse; they also encourage differences of emphasis, thereby providing "conditions favorable for theoretical development" (Danziger, 1990b, p. 332).

By discouraging metaphors and other figurative language, the *Manual* does the discipline a disservice. Metaphors are figures of thought as well as expression—if indeed that distinction can even be maintained. By discouraging metaphoric thought, traditional scientific style thereby discourages inventiveness, creativity, and theoretical development. Far from "distracting" readers from ideas, metaphors *are* ideas. Kurt Lewin said there is nothing so practical as a good theory; to this it may be added, there is nothing so theoretical as a good metaphor.

Brevity

When the *Manual* metaphorically asks psychologists to "weed out" superfluous language, it is continuing in the tradition of plain style that goes back at least three hundred years to Sprat's injunction against the "vicious abundance of Phrase" (1667/1959, p. 112). Sprat was reacting against the abundance of the Renaissance, when figures and ornaments were not just used, but overused and abused (Halloran & Bradford, 1984, p. 180). As we have seen, the status quo was a copious or Ciceronian style.

Yet styles are seldom culturally innocent. As Patricia Parker (1987, chap. 2) shows, during the Renaissance there was an association between style and gender, with "fat" dilated texts seen as feminine, and "lean" cryptic ones as masculine. The stereotyped opposition that was operating here is suggested by a Renaissance text: "Women are words, men deeds" (quoted by Parker, 1987, p. 22). The relationship between gender and writing was apparent to Erasmus, author of *De Copia*, who said that he was unable to find in Ciceronian eloquence anything that is "masculine" and spoke of his desire for a "more masculine" style (quoted by Parker, 1987, p. 14). Parker (1987) comments, "Ciceronian copia in these discussions is both effeminate and the style of a more prodigal youth, to be outgrown once one had become a man" (p. 14).

The association between style and gender presupposed an association between the body of the text and the human body—fat texts, fat people.

Parker traces the history of "literary fat ladies" from the Bible to Shake-speare. Even in modern times a character such as James Joyce's Molly Bloom follows in the tradition of the ample body and the dilated text. Parker's argument is that the classical arts of *copia* (abundance) and *dilatio* (delay, refusing to come to a point) are gendered issues. Throughout the history of literature they have been consistently associated with the feminine.

Turning the coin the other way, brevity in scientific writing can also be seen as a gendered issue. The lean, unadorned style favored for science is socially "masculine" just as the amplified, embellished style is socially "feminine." Thus the masculinist bias in academic discourse that we examined in Chapter 3—the privileging of one official genre—is also a stylistic question. The style most closely associated with masculinity is dominant; so-called feminine styles are marginalized, written off as dis-tracting.

If the amplified style has had few defenders in science, it has not had many more in composition studies. Composition specialists usually deal with expository prose, rather than scientific; but many plain-style values are common to both. Richard Lanham (1983) scornfully suggests that work in composition tends to be guided by a "C-B-S" theory of prose in which "clarity," "brevity," and "sincerity" are valued above all else.[18] Similarly, Phillip Arrington and Frank Farmer (1989)—in a review of three textbooks on style written by composition scholars—are critical of the books' preoccupation with "clarity," "concision," and "smooth reading" (p. 487).

Even so, it was not until Nevin Laib's (1990) article "Conciseness and Amplification" that amplified style received a serious discussion and defense. In Laib's account, amplification encompasses elaboration, expan-sion, emphasis, variation, paraphrase, restatement, and example.

Laib makes the point that amplification is often seen as a moral as well as a stylistic issue: "It is a sin to be superfluous" (p. 446). For our purposes, the sin of superfluity can be illustrated by an excerpt from the first edition of the APA *Manual* (American Psychological Association Council of Editors, 1952). "Brevity is important," the *Manual* said, "because it lightens the reader's burden,[19] reduces the costs of printing and editorial work, and serves to spread the limited space in the journals more widely among authors" (p. 10). In other words, to use more space than you strictly need is aggressive, wasteful, and selfish.

Indignation over needless amplification may be one reason for the frequent denunciations of "psychobabble," "doublespeak," "bureau-cratese," "bafflegab," and the like. Peter Madden and Lloyd Engdahl

(1973) satirize psychologists who produce fine-sounding but empty phrases. Madden and Engdahl developed the "EMPTI guide to swollen prose," a buzz-phrase generator that will add "bulk and a professional veneer" to psychologists' writing. EMPTI consists of three columns, each with fifteen terms; to produce a phrase, the writer selects at random one term from each column. The result is a *copia* of psychological language that would have impressed even Erasmus: "peripheral psychosocial adjustment," "undifferentiated empathic orientation," "diffuse cognitive integration," and more than 3,000 others.

The satire, surely, is justified. Haven't we all read texts that would have been more effective had they been more concise, had the writer taken time, in Strunk and White's phrase, to "omit needless words"? I agree with the *Manual* that wordiness *should* be "weeded out." Nevertheless, as Laib cautions, conciseness taken too far can become bluntness, opacity, and underdevelopment. After all, he asks, if an essay's point can be summarized in a few sentences or a thesis statement, and conciseness is the ideal, why say more? Psychologists might ask, If the gist of a paper can be conveyed in an abstract, and conciseness is the ideal, why write the paper?

Writers of psychology hear a lot about brevity but little about amplification. Journal editors, for instance, tend to dwell on the space-saving advantages of conciseness. Michael Pallak (1981), then editor of *American Psychologist*, said, "Most papers can be cut substantially, to their advantage" (p. 1474). On the other hand, Arthur Melton (1962), editor of the *Journal of Experimental Psychology*, noted a different reason for sending manuscripts back to authors for revision:

With a frequency that would surprise some readers, required revisions have consisted of *adding detailed description* of procedures, *making explicit* some design factor, *adding data* in tables or figures, and even urgings to the author[s] to *add words in order to make more explicit* [their] analysis and interpretations. (Melton, 1962, p. 555, emphasis added)

Thus development and explicit detail may be needed if the reader is to understand not simply the gist, but the texture of the writer's argument. Laib writes:

Amplification is useful and necessary. Restatement helps readers understand the concept. Those who do not grasp an idea when it is first articulated may understand it better when it is phrased differently or when the subject is described from a different perspective. Amplification reveals in greater detail the author's meaning. It fills in implications. It reduces the chance that an assertion will be

misunderstood. It emphasizes key points in the discussion, setting them apart
from less important information. (Laib, 1990, p. 449)

Thus amplification is teacherly; it is reader based. The *Publication
Manual* itself is a classic case of amplification, growing to thirty-two times
its original size between 1929 and 1983.

It is not Laib's intention, however, to replace the old prejudice against
amplification with a new one against conciseness. Conciseness and amplification are companion arts. Both are necessary; it is a matter of balance
and proportion.

Brevity shows respect for others, acknowledging how much their time is worth
and how small a claim to it one feels. Conciseness focuses the mind and reflects
concentration. . . . Amplification shows respect for the complexities and importance of the subject. It is patient with those who do not comprehend and generous
in explaining the author's point of view. (Laib, 1990, pp. 457–458)[20]

But "balance" and "proportion" are relative terms. Unlike the prescriptive and universal terms offered by the *Manual*, their meaning will vary
with different writers, readers, genres, texts, and occasions.

SUMMARY

I am not suggesting, then, that the present concise style favored by the
Manual be replaced by an amplified style. Nor, for that matter, am I
recommending that the ideal of clarity be abandoned, or that all empirical
reports feature metaphoric language. What I am suggesting is that we
investigate and challenge the assumptions of our charter documents. Just
as Ohmann's analysis of *The Elements of Style* leads to a reevaluation of
Strunk and White's classic handbook, so too does the work of Bazerman
and other composition scholars help us see the *Publication Manual* in a
new light.

The unstated assumptions of the *Manual* turn out to be tied to a number
of historical, linguistic, and even moralistic positions—positions that
psychologists may not necessarily be eager to adopt. Thus, to summarize,
the *Manual* advocates "clear" writing, but work within composition
studies suggests that "clarity" is a complex and problematic term, not least
because it implies a positivist, windowpane philosophy of language. The
Manual's distrust of metaphors and other "literary embellishments" also
needs to be challenged. Composition specialists have suggested that
figurative language is not out of place in scientific writing; this conclusion

is supported by work showing that metaphors continue to play an important role in psychological thought. Finally, scholars of rhetoric and composition can help us appreciate the historical precedents of plain style. Their work helps us understand why the modern taste for brevity should not be allowed to override the equally necessary art of amplification.

Chapter Five

Teaching Writing and Psychology

The human animal, as we know it, *emerges into personality* by first mastering whatever tribal speech happens to be its particular symbolic environment.

—Kenneth Burke (1966, p. 53)

In this book I have been using composition studies to develop a deeper understanding of writing in psychology. In the past, psychology's understanding of its own writing practices has been confined mainly to handbooks and student guides; considering writing from the perspective of composition enlarges our understanding of audience, genre, and style. In this new understanding, the generally single-voiced or monologic accounts of the handbooks are replaced by accounts that acknowledge dialogue and diversity. To summarize, a view of audience as anonymous and uniform is superseded by an understanding of diverse writer–reader relationships in psychological writing; a view of genre in which the empirical report is the only form worth mentioning is replaced by a view that acknowledges a multiplicity of genres; and a restrictive view of style as that authorized by the APA *Publication Manual* is overtaken by a broader, more tolerant understanding. Considering writing from the standpoint of composition studies thus enriches and makes more explicit our understanding.

What has been largely implicit so far, though, is what difference any of this might make. No doubt better understanding is a desirable goal in itself, but it is worth asking whether there are implications of this new understanding for actual practice. Or, to put it bluntly: So what? The purpose of this chapter is to address the "So what?" question.

As the chapter title suggests, in my view the most important implications have to do with teaching—how we present writing to our students. Therefore, in the following pages I will examine how teaching practices can be affected by reconceptualizations of audience, genre, and style. Before turning to a discussion of teaching, however, implications of genre and style for writing (and reading) practices should be briefly mentioned.

A revised understanding of genre and style would seem to call for changed practices both among those who write psychology and those who control publication outlets. Journal editors, publishers, referees, and reviewers determine what kinds of writing make it into print; they effectively define psychological discourse. Such gatekeepers have a responsibility to evaluate texts on their own terms, even if the texts are, by current standards, unconventional. The so-called feminized genres discussed in Chapter 3 would be far less marginalized if journal policies were revised so that these kinds of contributions were invited. Readers have a similar responsibility to take texts on their merits rather than according to preconceived notions of "proper" psychological discourse.

Furthermore, changes seem called for in psychology's charter documents—notably the APA *Manual*—that both reflect and shape our writing practices. The current edition leaves the impression that the empirical report is the only genre psychology needs. Much would be accomplished if, in the next revision of the *Manual*, due consideration were given to other genres, including feminized ones, because narrative, biography, and the exploratory essay are also legitimate forms of psychological writing. The *Manual* would also be more helpful if it were less "current-traditional" and more *rhetorical*—that is, if it acknowledged that every text is shaped by one's purposes, readers, and occasion as well as by one's content. Although the *Manual* will undoubtedly continue to prize clarity and brevity (and rightly so), clarity should be presented as a complex issue rather than as a simple property of texts, while brevity's companion art, amplification, should also be considered. Finally, the *Manual*'s discouragement of metaphors and other "poetic embellishments" ought to be revised in light of what we now know about scientific thought and writing. In brief, the present *Manual* does not accurately reflect the varieties of psychological discourse that currently exist; much less does it reflect the kinds of deeper understanding that we have gained from considering psychology's writing from the standpoint of scholarship in composition.

Nevertheless, I believe that the single most promising place to affect the discipline's writing practices is education, for the simple reason that, although not all students become psychologists, all psychologists were once students.[1] In other words, we need to think seriously about the ways writing is used in teaching, because it is while they are students that psychologists "emerge into personality," developing some of their deepest beliefs about what writing is and what it's for. In order to become psychologists, students need to learn not just how to write in a narrow skills sense. More fundamentally—and as I have tried to demonstrate in previous chapters—they need to learn that the vitality of the discipline depends on writing. Thus it is fitting that in a book about writing and psychology the final discussion should concern *teaching* writing and psychology.

Another reason it is appropriate to discuss teaching is that composition studies is closely associated with pedagogy. As mentioned in Chapter 1, composition has historically been identified with a single course in the college curriculum: "freshman comp." Whatever the reason, though, composition scholars seem attuned to teaching in a way that psychologists, in general, do not. For example, in theoretical articles on writing, authors frequently include more than a token discussion of educational implications. Needless to say, educational implications are not a standard feature of psychology articles, even though "intro psych" must be nearly as big an industry as freshman comp.

THE QUESTION OF CLASS SIZE

Drawing on the ideas presented in previous chapters, in this chapter I will suggest ways that psychology teachers could use writing in their undergraduate classes.[2] Of course, any suggestion that instructors might use more or different kinds of writing immediately raises the objection that psychology teachers often have very large classes. At the undergraduate level, class sizes of 100 or more are common; and in the introductory course, especially, sizes of 500 or even 1,000 are not unheard of. How can sustained writing be a serious component of such courses?

Although there are indeed ways (as discussed later) to incorporate writing, it is worth pointing out, first, that not everyone sees class size as a problem. James Jenkins (1991), for example, has defended large classes, especially for the introductory course, on the grounds that they offer economies of scale. Instead of paying more instructors to teach smaller classes, resources can be put into high-quality lectures (on film), tests, and auxiliary aids. As Jenkins readily admits, however, the argument holds only if the goal for the course is "the customary didactic one" and if achievement is measured "in conventional ways" (p. 77). Otherwise—if the goals for the course include "the development of skill in discussion, in argumentation, and in effective writing and the like" (p. 77)—large classes are less easily justified.

Effective writing *is* the main goal of writing courses, naturally, so the composition community has insisted on relatively small class sizes. The Conference on College Composition and Communication (1989) has endorsed the "Statement of Principles and Standards for the Postsecondary Teaching of Writing," which calls for a maximum of twenty students per class, or fifteen in a "developmental" class (p. 335). In practice, most composition classes probably have twenty to thirty students. But why does composition as a field limit classes to thirty, while psychology allows undergraduate classes of 100 or 500?

There is no simple answer. Certainly our large class sizes are partly a matter of tight budgets, but they are also a matter of disciplinary and institutional values that hold graduate teaching and research in greater esteem than undergraduate teaching (Russell, 1991, p. 295). If large class sizes are acceptable to the discipline as a whole, this suggests that psychology generally accepts the "customary didactic" goal of instruction. When the main goal of a course is to cover certain content, a lecture format is appropriate, even desirable (Jenkins, 1991).

Naturally, from their different perspective, writing teachers see things differently.[3] As Robert Brooke (1987b) explains, writing teachers try to help students view themselves as original thinkers rather than as "students" whose purpose is "to please teachers by absorbing and repeating information" (p. 152). One might say that writing teachers want their students to be writers first and students second. If psychology teachers wanted *their* students to be psychologists first and students second, we would, I suggest, need to revise some of our teaching practices: While content knowledge would still be valued very highly, more weight would be placed on original thinking and authoritative writing.

By subverting the traditional model of education, composition teachers challenge psychologists to reexamine our commitment to the lecture or transmission model of undergraduate education. This is not to say that psychology courses should be turned into writing courses. On the contrary, there are important differences between them because our goals *are* different. In addition to content knowledge, we want psychology students to develop skills and sensitivity in thinking, reading, listening, information gathering and synthesizing, research methods and statistics, ethics and values, interpersonal relations, and historical awareness (McGovern, Furumoto, Halpern, Kimble, & McKeachie, 1991). Nevertheless, because writing, in large part, is what psychologists do, it is particularly important that future psychologists also learn to be confident and effective writers. While the insights of composition teachers always need to be adapted to our own needs, psychology teachers would be well advised to listen carefully to those who specialize in the teaching of writing.

As mentioned earlier, writing teachers have one great advantage over psychology teachers: class size. Smaller classes would allow us to give more attention to writing, no doubt; but unfortunately there is no sign this is likely to happen soon. Therefore it is worth considering, at least briefly, how teachers who wish to do so can use writing even in large lecture classes.

One method is to pair the lecture class with a small, writing-intensive course. This is done, for instance, in the Writing Link program at the University of Washington. Although separately taught and graded, each Writing Link course follows closely the content and schedule of its companion lecture class (Russell, 1991, p. 288). A more common model is to turn large classes into small ones by having peer tutors or teaching assistants take over from time to time (Benjamin, 1991). The small classes could then be writing intensive even if the large classes were not.

Other less expensive options for encouraging writing and involvement include what Patricia Cross calls the "one-minute paper" (Light, 1990, p. 36): Near the end of class, students write down the big point learned that day as well as the main unanswered question they still have. The instructor reads these after class, using them as a starting point for the next lecture. Or, as suggested by Barbara Nodine (cited by Benjamin, 1991, p. 70), students could be asked to write an informal, ungraded answer to a discussion question at any time during the lecture, possibly exchanging their writing with adjacent classmates. In a related procedure, which James Reither calls *inkshedding*, students freewrite on a given topic, then exchange their writing with classmates (Coe, 1993; Paré, 1993). As they read one another's "inksheds," the students mark striking passages or entire texts, which are transcribed and published in time for the next class. Even in large classes, then, it is possible (although admittedly difficult) to create "an atmosphere . . . where writing is used, valued, and expected" (Russell, 1991, p. 289).

TEACHING PSYCHOLOGY WITHOUT WRITING

Before turning to a more detailed consideration of how psychology teachers could incorporate writing into their (smaller) classes, it is worth describing the present situation a little more closely. As noted earlier, undergraduate education in psychology often conforms to the *transmission model* of education in which a well-informed instructor delivers knowledge via lectures to large numbers of poorly informed students. This is what Paulo Freire (1970), in a well-known term, has labeled the "banking model," because teachers are seen as making deposits in their students' intellectual accounts.

Besides the lecture, the other most important elements in the transmission model are textbooks and tests. *Textbooks*—including psychology texts—have been widely criticized for bias, inaccuracies, and for reflecting commercial rather than academic interests.[4] Even so, the main problem with textbooks may well be how they are used in the classroom. Teachers tend to merge their authority with the authority of the book, and therefore students often take an uncritical stance toward both. Carmen Luke, Suzanne de Castell, and Allan Luke (1983) say that students assume "an acquiescent, *nonauthoritative status* in relation to both text and teacher" (p. 118), who themselves are "beyond criticism." When all classroom authority is vested in textbooks and teachers, however, it is difficult for students to see *themselves* as authorities and authors.

The transmission model lends itself to short-answer *tests*, because in this scheme knowledge tends to be seen as a commodity, a property that can be passed from one person to another. The widespread use in psychology of multiple-choice tests further implies that the discipline is a collection of indisputable facts. (There is always one right answer.) The concept of knowledge as an accumulation of discrete facts is consistent, too, with the notion of "incremental encyclopedism" that we considered in Chapter 4.[5]

If undergraduate education in psychology features lectures, textbooks, and short-answer tests, what is notably absent is sustained writing. And usually what writing does occur is for evaluation purposes. As James Britton and his colleagues found, students write in school primarily to display their knowledge to the teacher-as-examiner and earn a grade (Britton, Burgess, Martin, McLeod, & Rosen, 1975). Normally, the most that students in a one-semester psychology course would write is one, possibly two, single-draft term papers. Sometimes (and the probability increases with class size, of course) students would do no extended writing at all. Thus an opportunity is missed to show students that writing is both a way of learning and the chief means by which knowledge is constructed in the psychological community.

The low priority given to writing in psychology education is captured in an anecdote told by Thomas McGovern and Deborah Hogshead (1990) about Virginia Commonwealth University.

Five years ago, one of our department's outstanding undergraduate students told this story. After 52 semester hours of psychology, she had written only three papers; two were for [McGovern's] Psychology and Religious Experience course during her last semester at the university, the third was a formal research report for Experimental Methods. When she took an elective literature course in her senior year, the English faculty member took her aside after reviewing her initial papers and inquired about her writing experience. His assessment of her deficit stunned her. Fortunately, she had found in this faculty member a splendid mentor who began a crash course in bringing her to a college senior level of literacy. (McGovern & Hogshead, 1990, p. 5)

WRITING-ACROSS-THE-CURRICULUM PROGRAMS AND PSYCHOLOGY

The student's story prompted McGovern and Hogshead to learn more about composition studies; eventually McGovern became involved in his university's writing-across-the-curriculum (WAC) program. The WAC movement—one of composition's most successful "exports"—has helped sensitize psychologists and others to the value of writing.[6] Influenced by WAC, many psychologists have joined McGovern and Hogshead in thinking of writing as a verb (that is, as a process) rather than as a noun (a text to be corrected). Many have come to accept one of the basic tenets of the WAC approach, namely, that writing is not just a means of communicating ideas but is itself a powerful mode of learning (Emig, 1977).

The influence of WAC on psychology instruction is especially evident in the special issue of *Teaching of Psychology*, "Psychologists Teach Writing," edited by Barbara Nodine (1990). This issue has much useful discussion on the roles writing can play in psychology education. Articles about feedback, journals, faculty resistance, freewriting, and so on suggest that psychologists can be counted among the most enthusiastic supporters of WAC philosophy. On the other hand, several of the articles suggest that traditional disciplinary boundaries between psychology and composition are still firmly in place. Generally missing from the issue is a sense that the writing practices of psychology as a whole may be in need of revision and that we might look to composition studies as a source of ideas for such revision.

In fact, resistance or even hostility to composition studies occasionally surfaces, as it seems to, for instance, in Janina Jolley and Mark Mitchell's (1990) "Two Psychologists' Experiences with Journals." Although the idea for journals comes from composition, Jolley and Mitchell seem interested not in making connections but in drawing boundaries, distancing themselves from "English professors." According to Jolley and

Mitchell, these English professors use journals to promote students' "self-expression," whereas psychology teachers want *their* students "to ponder relevant psychological facts and theories."

We are indebted to English professors for introducing us to journals and giving us the benefits of their experiences. However, their experiences teaching students writing skills and self-expression are not entirely relevant to our situation. As psychology professors, we emphasize content rather than writing skills. Instead of encouraging students to express their own dogmatic beliefs, we want students to ponder other people's ideas. (Jolley & Mitchell, 1990, p. 40)

(Perhaps this is the reason, as Anne Herrington, 1992, observes, that psychology students often get the message that their own ideas and experience count for nothing—it's only "other people's ideas" that are important.)

While psychology teachers certainly have the right to adapt journal writing or any other activity to their own purposes, I'm concerned that we not misrepresent the aims of writing teachers. It's something of a caricature, I believe, to suggest that journal writing in composition classrooms is merely for the sake of "writing skills" and "self-expression." On the contrary, many compositionists view journal writing and freewriting as "writing-to-learn" activities; such writing affords the opportunity to come to a better understanding of something, to "figure things out" (Fulwiler, 1987b, p. 19).[7] Also problematic is the implication that students can meaningfully ponder other people's ideas without expressing (speaking or writing) them in their own language. It seems to me that Jolley and Mitchell are subscribing to the Ramist notion that ideas and expression can be cleanly separated (see Chapter 4). In any event, they seem to want to sharpen the differences between psychology and composition, whereas (I trust it is clear by now) my aim is to explore possible common ground.

Lorraine Nadelman's (1990) contribution to the *Teaching of Psychology* issue, "Learning to Think and Write as an Empirical Psychologist: The Laboratory Course in Developmental Psychology," also suggests a clear division between the two fields. Nadelman's students write sequential protocols of infant behavior, but writing like an empirical psychologist means that only certain kinds of statements are acceptable.

The observing and writing skills needed for sequential protocols is to provide *as many details as possible*, *as objectively as possible*, without obscuring the larger meaningful patterns. The student has to learn that if one writes "Johnny is angry," one is really making an inference about Johnny's behavior—which may or may not be accurate. The student has to learn to write, "Johnny's face flushed, his eyebrows . . . , his teeth clenched, he stamped his right foot," and so on. And in parentheses, the student may add "(he acted angry)"; the parentheses show the student's interpretation of behavioral events. (Nadelman, 1990, p. 45, emphasis added; ellipses in original)

What's interesting to me is the dichotomy between behavioral "facts" and subjective "interpretation," because from a different perspective the very *selection* of details would also be considered an act of interpretation. Also, recall Richard Ohmann's (1979) argument that focusing on details, in "definite, specific, concrete language," keeps students on the sensory surface of things, deflecting attention from more considered, analytic thought by which they try to understand a concept and relate it to other concepts (see Chapter 4).

It's apparent that Nadelman wants her students to write in "plain style"—an undeniably useful addition to anyone's repertoire. But if plain style is all they ever use, there is a danger that students could come to believe that writing is simply a matter of doing things the "one right way." Nadelman explains that, although the lab course in developmental psychology features a wide variety of topics and methods,

What does not vary . . . is the need for precise experimental reports, written in conventional publication style. This means that the organization is set, and the location of specific information is invariant. . . .

We emphasize that the style of writing throughout should be lucid, objective, and generally (but not always) lacking in subjective images and metaphors. The aim is to be clear, concise, and precise. Students who were accustomed to receiving As in high school English courses (and even deserving them) are initially flabbergasted to find our marginal notes, like "Repetitive," "Empty sentence," "Sentence too long and complex," "This can be said in half the words," and "Pretty, but what is its relevance to your point?" (Nadelman, 1990, p. 46)

As we have seen, however, a problem with asking students to aim for seemingly text-based qualities like clarity, concision, and precision is that it becomes more difficult to see writing as a social and rhetorical act—one that necessarily involves real readers. And in the reactions of the students who were "initially flabbergasted," can we not see something of the *imposition* of "conventional publication style"?

Emphasis on conventional scientific style acknowledges the importance of writing as a form of communication. The WAC movement, however, has made us more aware of how writing can also be a form of learning. In the remainder of this chapter I will suggest some ways psychologists can use writing—both as a form of learning and communicating—in their undergraduate teaching. Some of these ideas are from psychology teachers (often appearing in *Teaching of Psychology*); others are from composition specialists. Taken as a whole, the suggestions indicate that writing, while it is not everything, has an important part to play in the teaching of psychology. The general point I am making is that the teaching of writing in psychology must include, but should not be confined to, traditional scientific style.

IMPLICATIONS OF "AUDIENCE" FOR TEACHING PSYCHOLOGY

In *Writing Papers in Psychology: A Student Guide*, Ralph L. Rosnow and Mimi Rosnow (1986) tell students that they, as much as professional writers, need to "know your audience." Rosnow and Rosnow go on to say that "the audience is your instructor," and that therefore students should find out exactly what their instructor-audience wants (p. 5).

Based on the discussion in Chapter 2, however, it is difficult to accept the notion that "instructor" and "audience" are and should be one and the same. As we saw, the metaphor of *audience* implies that writing is a performance—an idea that psychologists would do well to go beyond. In fact, to quote Anthony Paré (1991), we might "usher out" the very idea of audience, replacing it with the more interactive metaphor of *conversation* or *dialogue* between writer and reader. What follows, then, are suggestions for revitalizing writer–reader relationships in the psychology classroom.

1. Consider not using the word *audience*—at least not in the monolithic sense. Instead we can think of multiple audiences or, even better, of the multiplicity of writer–reader relationships that are involved in any real writing situation. Thinking of texts as turns in a conversation rather than as performances helps deconstruct the idea of "audience." At a more modest level, simply using the word *readers* instead of *audience* directs attention to the real people who actually use a given piece of writing. But make-believe audiences and assignments "written to the void" discourage students from seeing the conversational, interactional nature of writing. Consider giving assignments in which students write to and for real audiences, because "nothing replaces a real audience as a stimulus to good writing and arguing" (Fahnestock, 1991, p. 191).

2. We don't have to evaluate everything. When every piece of writing is returned with a grade—whether it is polite applause (C) or a standing ovation (A+)—it inevitably gives the impression that writing is perform-ance. In other words, we can try to separate, if only some of the time, the teacher's roles of reader and evaluator. By always giving a grade we are

not acting as readers—at least not straightforward ones (Elbow, 1987). Teachers who always give feedback, make corrections, and assign grades are acting as "assessment machines"; some of the time we can be just readers, who respond, as in a letter (p. 65).[8] When teachers must be evaluators, they could hold off that role until the final draft; for early drafts they could be readers and responders. Virginia Chappell (1991) puts it succinctly: "The grading can wait" (p. 59).

Jack Selzer (1990) makes the related point that instructors too often are "unreal" readers: We read a piece of student writing even though we already know what it says. From a rhetorical standpoint this situation is extremely odd. Usually a writer has a need to say something and a reader has a need to find out; there's an imbalance between the two. Only, perhaps, in educational settings, where the main purpose of writing is evaluation, do we find writers who don't need to tell and readers who don't need to find out. Selzer recommends that students write small research reports or memos in which they write from a position of expertise and authority, telling the instructor things the instructor *genuinely wants and needs to hear*. Difficult as it is, this is one of the ways instructors can recast themselves as "real readers" rather than audiences.

3. As much as possible, consider having students write to and for real readers *other* than the instructor. They can write, on the one hand, to and for other "specialists": their classmates, textbook writers, journal editors. For example, students in my undergraduate cognitive psychology class once wrote letters to fourteen well-known cognitive psychologists, asking them about past accomplishments and current interests. The students received replies from most of them, and exceptionally detailed replies from some. Among other things, the students learned the important lesson that "big names" are also real people.

On the other hand, students can write to and for *non*specialist readers. Writing only for specialists (instructor or classmates) doesn't teach the "public dimensions and responsibilities of specialist knowledge" that writing to nonspecialists can (Fahnestock, 1986, p. 293). Students could write to (and get responses from) students in other classes, or they could explain psychological concepts to younger students. Herman Estrin (1981) had engineering students write books about science, ecology, hobbies, and engineering for grade-four children, while Paré (1991) had his engineering students write about physics for grade-eleven students (see also Ede & Lunsford, 1990, pp. 257–258).

Similarly, my introductory psychology class wrote a booklet about psychology for a grade-nine English class in a different city (MacDonald, 1993; Vipond, 1993). The psychology students were eager to correct the younger students' belief that psychology is only a helping profession. Therefore they focused on psychology as a science, writing about learning (for example, Pavlov, Watson, reinforcement) and memory (Ebbinghaus, Bartlett, eyewitness testimony). The psychology students' task was compelling because they were writing not for an abstract audience, but for real readers with real beliefs and misconceptions.

The purpose of having students write for different readers is that they will learn about the subject as well as learning about writing. A student doing empirical research on the moral development of young children learns something by writing a report for her professor and classmates. She will learn something else about her project, however, when she writes an explanatory letter to the parents—or to the children themselves.

4. We can have students practice "document cycling." Instead of asking for a single-draft term paper, we can ask for two or more drafts, making comments on each. Or, students could exchange drafts, comment on them, and talk to one another about them. In this way writers can begin to understand how their writing affects readers. Reader response leads to *revision*, which should be understood not simply as copy editing, but as the "deeper intellectual penetration of a subject through additional composing, even to the point of repudiating earlier formulations altogether" (Knoblauch & Brannon, 1984, p. 131).

5. Consider ways to demonstrate that writing is social action rather than performance. For example, students can interact with one another and the instructor through writing. Computers have made it possible as never before to "talk" in writing. Local area networks, bulletin boards, and e-mail allow teachers to recreate the classroom as an "online discourse community" (Trent Batson, quoted by Hawisher & Selfe, 1991, p. 57) in which ideas and information are exchanged in nontraditional ways.[9] We need to think carefully about how technology can improve the educational spaces we and our students inhabit (Hawisher & Selfe, 1991, p. 64). More specifically, we need to understand how computers can assist our students (and ourselves) do things with writing.

6. Put textbooks in their place. As mentioned earlier, the main problem with textbooks may be how they are used. Used uncritically, as supremely authoritative documents, textbooks function as conversation stoppers. If, on the other hand, textbooks are used as resource materials—and are seen as just as interested and rhetorically based as any other writing—they can be exceptionally useful for students' writing and learning projects. I like to keep textbooks in my classes at the back of the room or in the library where, along with abstracts, dictionaries, and other resources, they can be consulted rather than studied. Another possibility is to make the textbook

the central feature of the course, "problematizing" it. For example, students could critically examine the book's assumptions or coverage, or consider how the authors appropriate source material.

7. We can seek ways to engage students in the ongoing conversations of psychology. Composition specialists such as David Bartholomae (1985) and Kenneth Bruffee (1984) argue that the role of education is not to dispense knowledge, but to induct new members into knowledge communities. Writing teachers and psychology teachers have different goals to some extent; even so, how can we, as Kenneth Burke (1973) would say, help students "put their oar in"?

In composition studies, the kinds of teaching practices known by the generic term *collaborative learning* go at least partway toward this goal. Collaborative learning—which encompasses reader response, peer critiques, small writing groups, joint writing projects, and peer tutoring (Trimbur, 1985, p. 87)—challenges the traditional, hierarchically organized classroom in which knowledge is passed down from teacher to student.[10] As John Trimbur (1985) explains, learning in the collaborative classroom is a product of students' social relations with one another:

In the traditional teacher-centered classroom, the students are atomized; they are an aggregate of individuals organized to learn from and perform for the teacher as individuals. In contrast to this model, collaborative learning attempts to decentralize the authority traditionally held by the teacher and to shift the locus of knowledge from the sovereign domain of the teacher to the social interaction of the learners. (Trimbur, 1985, p. 89)

Collaborative learning goes against the grain of psychology education, which tends to be organized on a hierarchical, knowledge-transmission model. Nevertheless, if, as argued in Chapter 2, psychology is a knowledge and discourse community, then psychology students need "to learn, from the inside, its major questions, its governing assumptions, its language, its research methods, its evidential contexts, its forms, its discourse conventions, its major authors and its major texts—that is, its knowledge and its modes of knowing" (Reither, 1985, p. 624).

The operative phrase here is "from the inside." James Reither and I suggested that in order to help students learn from the inside it is necessary to rethink the term *collaboration* (Reither & Vipond, 1989). We distinguished three senses of collaboration—as coauthoring, workshopping, and knowledge making—and we recommended that courses, including psychology courses, be made collaborative in all three ways. First, coauthoring and team writing assignments can be included as normal, everyday activities. Second, the classroom can function as a "workshop" in which the students write to and for their peers and respond to one another's work. Third, and most important, the whole course or a component of it can be conceived as a scholarly or scientific research project in order to give students the opportunity to engage in genuine inquiry.[11]

When students are recast as active inquirers ("conversationalists") rather than as containers for knowledge, they learn how social and collaborative their writing and learning projects necessarily are. And writing from the standpoint of a conversationalist is a different proposition entirely from writing in order to demonstrate knowledge to one's instructor.

IMPLICATIONS OF GENRE FOR TEACHING PSYCHOLOGY

As we saw in Chapter 3, psychologists write in a great number of different genres. There is, however, a hierarchy of genres, with the empirical report considered superior to all the rest. Similarly, psychology students usually do just two kinds of writing. In survey courses, they tend to write term papers or research papers; in lab courses, they write empirical reports.

In order to demonstrate the diversity of genres that psychologists actually use, instructors should expand the range of genres that students read and write. As well as learning the "masculinist" discourse of traditional science and the academy, students should learn the "feminist" discourses of narrative, autobiography, and the exploratory essay. Writing in these different genres requires different modes of knowing and thus affords the opportunity for new and expanded kinds of learning. Here again are some concrete suggestions.

1. Consider having students use a range of genres in their writing. Then, rather than basing grades on just one or two pieces of writing, ask for a *portfolio* that contains different types.

Some teachers are understandably reluctant to introduce more writing into their classrooms because they don't have time to mark extra assignments. With portfolio evaluation, however, the teacher does not necessarily have to grade (or even read) everything; instead, students select their best work and submit this sample as their portfolio.[12]

Portfolio evaluation was used, for example, by Susan Beers (1985), who had students write a total of ten to fifteen pages for a one-semester course in life-span development. The students themselves decided what kinds of writing would make up this total: autobiographical essays, in-class exercises, out-of-class observations, book reviews, article reports, short stories, poems. Most of the writing was submitted first in draft form and graded only at the end.

2. We can encourage nonacademic as well as academic discourse. Naturally we want students to learn how to think and write "like a psychologist," and we do all we can to encourage them to join the discourse communities of psychology. But perhaps we should be more concerned whether students can make sense of their reading and experience, and less concerned whether they can tell what belongs in the results section of a paper and what belongs in the discussion. We need to remember that most undergraduates do not become psychologists; possibly, in the larger scheme, there are more important things to learn than APA style. As Peter Elbow (1991) says, "life is long and college is short" (p. 136). Besides teaching academic discourse, then, we should give some consideration to its nonacademic cousins.

What is *nonacademic discourse*? For Elbow, it is a type of writing in which one clarifies claims and gives reasons. In nonacademic discourse, one takes on "the admirable larger intellectual tasks like giving good reasons and evidence yet doing so in a rhetorical fashion which acknowledges an interested position and tries to acknowledge and understand the positions of others" (p. 148). Thus nonacademic discourse is not nonintellectual discourse.

It is, however, relatively free of the jargon and hedging often found in the academic species. An advantage is that it's easier then to tell if students really know what they're talking about. Elbow says, "Using the vernacular helps show whether the student is doing real intellectual work or just using academic jive" (p. 149).

Instructors can encourage students to write in the vernacular by having them, for instance, write *letters* in addition to essays and term papers. Kerry Chamberlain and Stephen Burrough (1985) had cognitive psychology students write a critique of a published article in the form of a letter to someone naive in that area (parents, spouse, or a friend). Using everyday language, the students explained the background of the article, described new insights, related the article's knowledge claim to other knowledge, and discussed applications. Similarly, John Charlesworth and John Slate (1986) had developmental psychology students write fictional letters to a preadolescent son or daughter, in language the children would understand. The letters discussed the changes the children could expect to experience at puberty. Charlesworth and Slate found the assignment valuable because it not only "covered the content," but also increased the students' comfort in talking about sensitive topics. (The exercise may also have shown who was doing "real intellectual work" and who was merely using "academic jive.") And in his Current Advances in Psychology course, Timothy Osberg (1991) had students read articles from *American Psychologist*, *Psychological Bulletin*, and *Annual Review of Psychology*, as well as watch videotapes. Near the end of term, students wrote an integrative paper "in a format that would be appropriate for a popular periodical, such as *Time*, to inform the average American about recent advances in the field" (Osberg, 1991, p. 41).

The use of nonacademic, everyday language in these assignments is a useful adjunct to the genre-limited academic writing found in most classrooms. Nevertheless, these assignments would have been even more powerful, in my view, if they didn't have a fictional, "as if" quality. For example, instead of having students pretend they're writing for *Time*, why not have them actually write for the real readers of their campus paper—or publish their own anthology?[13]

3. We can seek ways to include a particular kind of nonacademic discourse: discourse that *renders* rather than *explains* experience. Experience is explained in academic essays and reports, rendered in journals, diaries, logs, dialogues, poetry, fiction, autobiographies, and biographies.[14]

Some psychologists may be uncomfortable with the idea of using creative writing in the classroom. Literature, fiction, and narrative belong in the English class, but they seem out of place in scientific psychology. But *genre blurring* as well as the growing interest in narrative psychology have turned these convenient boundaries into contested sites. Humans seem to have a need "to story," whether the stories told are literary or scientific ones.[15] Furthermore, the discussion in Chapter 3 suggests that the bias against (or fear of) literary and experiential modes of understanding is part of the masculinist tradition of mainstream science. By incorporating creative writing in the curriculum, then, psychology teachers may contribute to a much larger, emancipatory project.

An example of how creative writing could be used in psychology is provided by Michael Gorman, Margaret Gorman, and Art Young (1986). A major objective of Michael Gorman's introductory psychology course was "to get students to see schizophrenia from the inside—to understand what it means to be schizophrenic, not just to memorize a series of facts about schizophrenia" (p. 140). To this end Gorman had his students write poems and short stories as well as traditional papers about schizophrenia. Thus the students not only learned about different perspectives on schizophrenia (for example, biomedical versus humanistic-existential); to some extent they experienced them, seeing schizophrenia "from the inside."

4. Consider exploiting the distinction between explaining and rendering experience. Students can be asked to use both modes, even in the same paper. This implies a kind of genre mixing that, again, runs against the grain of standard academic discourse. Even so, psychology instructors could encourage papers such as the one completed by Ms. W (Bleich, 1989). It may be recalled from Chapter 3 that Ms. W, a student in a graduate criticism course, started with a conventional analysis of a text and then wrote a less formal narrative that clarified why she had chosen the text in the first place. Or, psychologists might adopt Elbow's (1991) two-step proposal (p. 150). The first step is to ask for a piece of writing that renders something from experience; the second is to ask for a different piece of writing that builds on that writing—an essay that explains some issue or solves a conceptual (not a personal) problem. Similarly, Rebecca Stoddart and Ann Kimble Loux (1992) recommend "two-tiered" papers. Their psychology students begin by writing personal narratives and only then conduct relevant research, adding documentation as required. Of all the disciplines, psychology seems especially well suited to such a scheme.

IMPLICATIONS OF STYLE FOR TEACHING PSYCHOLOGY

Although psychologists and their students should be able to use a variety of genres, none of this is meant to imply that we can afford to neglect the traditionally dominant genre: the empirical report. Even if it's one among many, laboratory rhetoric will continue to have an important place in psychology's writing and learning projects. Therefore teachers of psychology will almost certainly want their students—especially advanced ones—to learn APA style. However, this leaves open the question of *how* to teach it, because there are several possibilities.

Usually, style conventions are taught as a matter of correctness. From this angle the APA *Manual* is seen as a book of etiquette that prescribes dos and don'ts. A single form is held up as the ideal to which all writing aspires; any text that falls short is returned with its errors marked in red. Seen as a matter of right and wrong, style conventions need to be learned, but the rules themselves don't merit serious discussion—they're just there. This seems to be the thinking behind the document *Mastering APA Style* (Gelfand & Walker, 1990), which, according to a page five APA advertisement in its April 1991 *Monitor*, "reduces the need for detailed instruction . . . and leaves professors more time to teach course material."

In composition, this formalist approach to style—current-traditional rhetoric—has been a force in literacy instruction since the late nineteenth century (Crowley, 1990). Not the least of its drawbacks, however, is that it makes a discipline into an exclusive club and a teacher into a gatekeeper, preventing students from entering unless they know the magic words, or, in this case, the magic citation format. This is the old game of right and wrong in which "the student's whole task is finding right answers of which the teacher is sole arbiter" (Elbow, 1991, p. 151). In the following paragraphs, I offer suggestions for ways of teaching (not training) APA style that go beyond the current-traditional.

1. Consider teaching style as a matter of reader expectations. Suppose, for instance, that an instructor asked for two versions of a research report: one suitable for the *Journal of Experimental Psychology*; the other suitable for *Scientific American*. Wouldn't students then learn some important lessons not only, for instance, about forms of citation, but about *motives* for citation? Teaching style as a matter of reader expectations means that students are encouraged to keep asking, Why am I doing this? What effect will this have on readers? And it leads quite naturally to trying out drafts on real readers.

2. Consider teaching style contrastively. Psychology students rightly want to learn APA style because it's seen as a key to success. Nevertheless, instructors could help students learn to *analyze* conventional style and see the unconventional as possibly effective in given situations (S. Miller, 1991, p. 112). One way to do this would be to teach APA style in conjunction with Modern Language Association style (Gibaldi & Achtert, 1988) or University of Chicago style (Turabian, 1987), having students experience the advantages and limitations of each. A contrastive approach—supplemented by a careful reading of Bazerman's (1988) work—would help students understand how the stylistic conventions adopted by psychology both enable and constrain different kinds of knowing. Instead of simply asserting rules, we should help students reflect on them, help them understand that particular epistemologies are embedded in APA and other styles (Herrington, 1992). A contrastive approach would help students understand that "rules" are actually rhetorical practices and are therefore open to change (Dias, Beer, Ledwell-Brown, Paré, & Pittenger, 1992, pp. 151–152).

3. We can have students write empirical reports using ad-hoc headings as well as in standard IMRAD (introduction-method-results-and-discussion) form. The standard format lets writers off too easily. Ad-hoc headings—chosen according to the nature of the argument and one's purposes, readers, and occasion—invite writers to make transitions between sections, show relationships, and decide for themselves what should be included under particular headings (Bazerman, 1988). Journals such as

Science, *Nature*, and *Physical Review* use ad-hoc headings, so there seems to be no reason in principle that psychology students couldn't, at least some of the time, do the same.

4. Get clear about "clarity." As discussed in Chapter 4, clarity is not a property of texts but is used as a synonym for "effective" and "successful"; it drags some questionable philosophical baggage along with it, too. We must continue to encourage students to write clearly. Even so, we need to remember that clarity is in the mind of the reader, not in the text. Examining the difficult concept of clarity may open the door to the larger question of how psychologists exploit linguistic resources to make knowledge claims. Discussion could help students see the extent to which scientific papers are not transcriptions of reality but rhetorical actions intended to move and bend people to action, belief, and attitude (Burke, 1950/1969). In short, we can help students understand that a reason for writing is to take part in a communal knowledge-making process, not just to make one more deposit in the "repository" of psychological information.

5. We can resist "literaphobia" by examining how psychologists (including even the writers of the APA *Manual*) routinely use so-called literary language to relate ideas to one another. For instance, metaphors are not mere poetic embellishments, but are an essential part of thought; they belong as much to rhetorical *invention* as to *style*. Boundaries between "literary" and "scientific" language can be usefully blurred by having students read and write about stylists of science such as Rachel Carson, Loren Eiseley, and Oliver Sacks.

6. As well as valuing conciseness, we can also value its companion virtue, amplification. By teaching the values of both conciseness and amplification, we can help students "strike a balance that fits the occasion" (Laib, 1990, p. 457).

CONCLUSION

Drawing on composition studies—especially the WAC movement—in the preceding pages I have suggested some ways psychology teachers could use writing more fully. Although these are not definitive lists, I have emphasized teaching for two reasons. First, as mentioned before, all psychologists were once students, so the *discipline's* attitudes to writing are powerfully shaped by the ways writing is conceived in education. Second, because psychology is steeped in writing (Chapter 1), it follows that students who are capable and confident writers will become better psychologists. Writing is central to psychology and just as central to education.

A tacit theme of this book is that psychology could learn a great deal from other disciplines. But if we are to learn from composition studies or any other field, we need to converse with those beyond our borders. As John Clifford (1991) says, "The crucial idea here is to be the questioning subject, not the subject who already knows. Struggling effectively at work to rewrite the dominant discourse, to refigure the curriculum, and to rework received notions of subjectivity, we help to loosen the grip of the hegemonic" (p. 194).

Teachers, students, researchers, theorists, journal editors, reviewers, publishers, and organizations can all "help to loosen the grip of the hegemonic" in psychology's writing and teaching practices. They can do so by recognizing the diversity of writer–reader relationships rather than privileging a single performer–audience relationship, and by encouraging a range of genres and styles rather than idolizing a single type of "masterful" academic writing.

As we saw in Chapter 1, from the early 1960s the current of influence has run from psychology to composition: Composition specialists have appropriated numerous concepts and methods from psychology. In subsequent chapters, we saw what could happen if, reversing the polarity, psychology were to use composition to enrich its understanding of audience, genre, style, and teaching. Understanding writing and teaching from the perspective of composition studies makes evident composition's diversity and open-mindedness—a refusal to be dominated by a single, unifying discourse. This may even be one of composition's defining characteristics. Addressing the Conference on College Composition and Communication, David Bartholomae said:

To propose a unifying tradition, a canon, disciplinary boundaries—to do this is to turn our backs on our most precious legacy, which is a willed and courageous resistance to the luxury of order and tradition. The charge to this generation and the next is to keep the field open, not to close it; to provide occasions for talk, not lecture and silence; . . . to resist the temptations of rank and status. (Bartholomae, 1989, p. 49)

I don't think psychology can easily be characterized as demonstrating "a willed and courageous resistance to the luxury of order and tradition." On the contrary, the history of our discipline has been a story of, if anything, too much order: firm disciplinary boundaries and, as Kurt Danziger (1990a) argues, a premature closing-off of other possibilities. Although psychology is highly diverse in what it studies, in its writing it has tended to embrace a "unifying tradition" that discourages alternate forms and styles. As I have tried to show throughout this book, psychology could usefully look to composition studies as a model for keeping its writing and teaching practices open (not closing them), providing occasions for talk (not lecture and silence), and resisting the temptations of rank and status. But models—even good ones—can take us only so far. Scholarship in composition provides psychology with a fresh understanding of writing and its teaching, but what happens now that the ball is back in our court? Can we act on our understanding?

Notes

CHAPTER 1

1. As far as I know, the term *composition studies* was first used in print by Robert Connors (1983a). Context permitting, in this book the terms *composition* and *composition studies* will be used interchangeably.

2. The situation is different in Canada, which has a strong tradition of belles lettres (see Buitenhuis & Coe, 1988). Here, composition is less likely to be a separate course and more likely to be taught as part of an English "lit/comp" package. Even so, the number of writing courses and programs in Canada is increasing (Graves, 1991).

3. Some of the main journals in composition are *College Composition and Communication, College English, Journal of Advanced Composition, Research in the Teaching of English, Rhetoric Review*, and *Written Communication*. The most important serial bibliography is the *CCCC Bibliography of Composition and Rhetoric*. For discussion, see Robert Connors (1984) and Patrick Scott (1991).

4. Alternatively, it could be said that composition courses indoctrinated students into the linguistic conventions and capitalist values of the dominant class (Slevin, 1991). The first-year composition course served (and serves?) a "winnowing" function, as well (S. Miller, 1991, p. 63), "weeding out those deemed inappropriately prepared to enter the various 'communities' that make up the university" (Slevin, 1991, p. 151). To say the least, the first-year composition course continues to be a site of controversy and political struggle (Bullock, Trimbur, & Schuster, 1991; Hairston, 1992).

5. For Eliot in 1879, learning to write in the vernacular was an important part of a college education. "I recognized but one mental acquisition as an essential part of the education of a lady or a gentleman—namely, an accurate

and refined use of the mother tongue" (quoted by Russell, 1991, p. 50). In 1900 the first-year writing course became the only required course at Harvard (p. 50).

6. Today, with a membership of approximately 7,500, CCCC is the organizational home base for most composition specialists. By comparison, APA has 118,000 members and the Canadian Psychological Association (CPA) has about 4,000. However, only about twenty percent and twenty-five percent of members attend the annual meetings of APA and CPA, respectively, whereas fifty percent of CCCC members attend their meetings.

7. As Sharon Crowley (1990) explains, the curious term *current-traditional*—coined by Daniel Fogarty in 1959—captures the fact that a fairly coherent set of practices has dominated the teaching of writing "over a remarkable stretch of time" (p. 175).

8. British educators such as James Britton and John Dixon understood "process" differently from their American counterparts (Britton, Burgess, Martin, McLeod, & Rosen, 1975; Dixon, 1967). For the Americans (following Bruner), process tended to refer to the way a school subject was taught; whereas for the British (following Piaget and Vygotsky), it meant the development or growth of the child (Harris, 1991). American and British educators learned about one another's work in 1966 at the Dartmouth Seminar (the Anglo-American Conference on the Teaching of English).

9. Although my concern in this section is to show how compositionists have used psychology, it should be noted that psychologists, too, have recognized the therapeutic benefits of freewriting, self-expressive writing, and "journaling" (e.g., Progoff, 1975). James Pennebaker (1991) argues that self-expressive writing can improve physical as well as psychological health.

10. The implication that American psychology has, or at least had, imperialistic designs is not without foundation. For most of the twentieth century—Kurt Danziger (1990a) writes—"American psychologists were able to exploit the special congruence of their founding myth with the 'American ideal' to assert imperialistic claims over many other areas of human knowledge" (p. 194). As Danziger notes, Joseph Jastrow, Edward Thorndike, and James McKeen Cattell were among those arrogant enough to claim that, of all the human sciences, psychology was or should be the "master" (p. 248).

11. Robert Connors (1984) argues that this was "an important declaration of allegiance; with that seemingly small change Purves [the editor] announced that *RTE* was moving fully into the orbit of social-science research and away from the humanities tradition implied by the MLA [Modern Language Association] style" (p. 355). Other writing and English journals that have since adopted APA style are *Language Arts*, *English Quarterly*, and the interdisciplinary *Written Communication*.

CHAPTER 2

1. Peter Elbow (1987), however, argues that at times writers do and should ignore their audiences. For example, journal writing and writing-to-learn assign-

ments (as in writing-across-the-curriculum, or WAC, classrooms) are for the self or possibly for no one at all, not for an outside reader. The point of such writing, Elbow says, is not the writing but the new thoughts, feelings, and understanding that the writing produces. Writers can discover their meaning through writing: "You throw away the writing, often unread, and keep the mental changes it has engendered" (p. 59). Elbow's argument is a useful reminder that not all writing aspires to a public forum. Nevertheless, in most discussions of audience, including this chapter, it is assumed that the writer is planning to "go public," whether in a scientific journal, an interoffice memo, or a term paper.

2. From a different perspective, audience can be seen as an "invoked" entity, which refers to the audience "called up or imagined by the writer" (Ede & Lunsford, 1984, p. 156n). Most often, *invoked audiences* refer to readers of literary works (Gibson, 1950; Ong, 1975), but Gay Gragson and Jack Selzer (1990) suggest that writers of scientific articles also invoke or fictionalize their audiences. I take a different approach in this chapter.

3. For an introduction to this area, see, in addition to the works discussed in the text, the edited collections of Charles Bazerman and James Paradis (1991), Carolyn Matalene (1989), Lee Odell and Dixie Goswami (1985), Charles Sides (1989), and Rachel Spilka (1993). There are several journals devoted to writing and teaching writing in the workplace, including the *Journal of Business and Technical Communication*, the *Journal of Technical Writing and Communication*, *Management Communication Quarterly*, and the *Technical Writing Teacher*.

4. *Inscription*—the "encoding of experience in socially validated symbols" (Winsor, 1989, p. 271)—is the process by which physical reality is given symbolic form (as numbers, graphs and curves, published papers, and so on). Scientific research entails a chain of inscriptions because later documents "refer to and are based on other documents" (Winsor, 1990, p. 60). Winsor's discussion of inscription draws on Bruno Latour and Steve Woolgar (1986, p. 51), who in turn borrow from Jacques Derrida (1976).

5. The idea that readers as well as writers make meaning is now almost a truism, but it wasn't when reader-response theorists such as Louise Rosenblatt (1938/1976) first said it. Now, as Louise Wetherbee Phelps (1985) says, "the composing and reading processes are no longer distinct. The reader's perspective is bound up in the writing process itself, . . . while intended meanings are only fully realized through a reader's comprehension" (p. 14). In general, composition specialists have tended not to recognize the importance of reader-response and other reader research for their work on audience; for an exception, see Helen Rothschild Ewald (1991).

6. The interactional nature of academic writing is apparent in other ways, as well. Greg Myers (1989), who has studied the writing of biologists, argues that many features of scientific writing that are usually regarded as matters of convention (for instance, use of the passive voice) are better explained as matters of "politeness" and "face"—that is, are better explained interactionally.

7. "Discourse community" became a dominant concept in composition during the 1980s, but, as Paré (1991) observes, "no widely accepted definition has emerged. In fact, like 'audience,' the term is likely to resist precise definition and thus gain connotative power" (p. 61n). For further discussion of discourse communities, see David Bartholomae (1985), Patricia Bizzell (1982), Marilyn Cooper (1989), James Porter (1986), and John Swales (1990, chap. 2).

CHAPTER 3

1. Similarly, Carolyn Miller (1984) observes that the set of genres "is an open class, with new members evolving, old ones decaying" (p. 153). Consequently, "the number of genres current in any society is indeterminate and depends upon the complexity and diversity of the society" (p. 163).

2. The *Manual* misses some genres, such as obituaries, that *are* regularly published in APA (and other) journals. Although often overlooked, obituaries are an important form of "epideictic" or ceremonial discourse, "composed in order to celebrate or reaffirm community values" (Crowley, 1990, p. 157).

3. According to Donald Foss (1985), as late as 1975 the appearance of reviews of single-author books were nearly three times as common as reviews of edited anthologies; ten years later they were less common. Lois Granick (1989) notes that edited collections accounted for thirty-five percent of the 1,856 books received by PsycINFO Services (APA's information clearinghouse) in 1988.

4. It may be wondered whether memos and term papers, for instance, ought to be dignified with the term *genre*. My approach follows that of Carolyn Miller (1984), who argues that these everyday, de-facto discourse types should indeed be considered genres because they "tell us something theoretically important about discourse" (p. 155).

To consider as potential genres such homely discourse as the letter of recommendation, the user manual, the progress report, the ransom note, the lecture, and the white paper, as well as the eulogy, the apologia, the inaugural, the public proceeding, and the sermon, is not to trivialize the study of genres; it is to take seriously the rhetoric in which we are immersed and the situations in which we find ourselves. (Miller, 1984, p. 155)

5. Skinner wasn't the only psychologist to write a utopian work; he was preceded by G. Stanley Hall, William McDougall, Hugo Münsterberg, and J. B. Watson (Morawski, 1982). Skinner studied English as an undergraduate, and after graduation he spent a year trying to write fiction. Donald Hebb had a similar ambition. In his autobiography, Hebb (1980) says that as an undergraduate he intended to be a novelist; unfortunately, after graduating he never got as far as even a first draft. Hebb goes on to say that Skinner could get the fiction out of his system with *Walden Two*, but "for me, as others have observed, it had to be *The Organization of Behavior*" (Hebb, 1980, p. 273).

6. According to David Russell (1991), empirical reports and other research-oriented genres became required for students in the late nineteenth century, at the same time the "research ideal" was being instilled in faculty. By casting

suspicion on all genres that weren't properly "academic," the research ideal effectively narrowed the range of genres students could write in. "In short," says Russell, "student writing was conceived in the image of faculty writing" (p. 74).

7. *Psychological Review, Psychological Bulletin,* and *American Psychologist* are consistently near the top of every list, regardless of whether the list is derived from citation impact (Buffardi & Nichols, 1981; Feingold, 1989; Matson, Gouvier, & Manikam, 1989) or subjective ratings (Koulack & Keselman, 1975).

8. Murray White (1983) identified the fifty most frequently cited publications in cognitive psychology from 1979 to 1982. Of these, twenty-six were chapters or books; of the twenty-four journal articles, thirteen were published in *Psychological Review* or *Psychological Bulletin* or were otherwise nonconventional (for example, imagery norms). At most, therefore, eleven (or 22 percent) were traditional, journal-length empirical reports. Of the thirty-two publications cited in a majority of perception textbooks, sixteen were chapters or books (White, 1987); at most, 40 percent of the publications were conventional research reports.

9. Susan Peck MacDonald (1987) argues, following Stephen Toulmin, that different disciplines differ in their approach to problems. At one end of the continuum are the sciences, where problems are relatively few in number, readily discernible, generalizable, and communal; at the other end are the humanities, where problems are far less constrained and conventionalized. MacDonald places the social sciences, including psychology, much closer to the sciences than to literary interpretation and other humanities.

10. Reviewers, take note.

11. The contrast between competitive and noncompetitive approaches to science is nicely captured by Max Wertheimer in his tribute to Carl Stumpf in 1918. Some psychologists, said Wertheimer, "approach nature as an enemy; they set up traps and try to defeat her, or they are like sportsmen who want to show off their own skill and strength." Turning to Stumpf he asked, "How different are you?" To illustrate Stumpf's method, Wertheimer made this analogy: "With one African tribe there exists the following custom: When they want to show a guest that they trust him, a mother puts a baby into his arms and says, 'Hold the child.' That is how you hold the facts in your hands, and that you have taught us, reverence for reality" (as told by Heider, 1970, p. 135).

12. Similarly, arguing from a unification perspective, Arthur Staats (1991) decries the numerous schisms in psychology (between nature and nurture, for instance).

In our modern disunified science the typical approach is to take one side of the schism, attempt to enhance it, and discredit the other side—the discreditation then being taken as further support. Much energy is expended and wasted in such arguments. When this process is considered, it can be seen to be quite strange, inasmuch as productive research, methods, findings, and theory are typically found on each side. (Staats, 1991, p. 906)

13. The discussion of academic writing by compositionists has some parallels with the discussion of individualism in psychology. Edward Sampson (1988), for instance, contrasts two indigenous psychologies: "self-contained" and "ensembled" individualism. Citing Morton Deutsch's work on cooperation and competition, Sampson observes that an emphasis on individual achievement may thwart long-term cultural success, as separate, self-contained actors each strive for a place in the sun. On the other hand, "when persons' sense of self is defined through relationship and connection, achievements will occur, not from separate actors seeking somehow to mesh their behavior together, but rather from thoroughly interdependent actors whose very design for being includes working on behalf of larger interests" (Sampson, 1988, p. 21). Thus it is possible to link adversarial thinking with self-contained individualism, and Burke's "cooperative competition" with Sampson's ensembled individualism.

14. Some monastic traditions were carried over to universities when they became the new centers of learning. For example, at one time the professors at Oxford and Cambridge were not allowed to marry (Schiebinger, 1989); in fact, "until late into the nineteenth century celibacy was required of all faculty" (p. 151).

15. According to Janis Bohan (1990), the reasons for women's relative invisibility in psychology are many, ranging from outright discrimination such as Titchener's to practices as subtle as the current APA reference citation system (see Chapter 4), where only initials of first names are used in reference lists. Not giving first names, however, means that women's contributions cannot be identified and thus the presumption of male authorship is left unchecked (Bohan, 1990, p. 85). Bohan therefore uses full names for all authors—a practice I follow in this book as well (cf. Walsh-Bowers, 1992). Notice that the initials-only style is also exclusionary in Elbow's sense: First names aren't necessary because insiders already know who these people are (R. Hunt, personal communication). Interestingly, though, from about 1945 to 1965 APA style mandated initials for male authors only; women were cited by their full first names. The APA *Manuals* of 1952 and 1957 were also careful to note, "For married women, use the name as given in the publication cited" (American Psychological Association Council of Editors, 1952, p. 44).

16. It is particularly appropriate to turn to composition studies for discussions of feminized genres, because composition itself has often been identified as a feminized field of studies (Flynn, 1988; Holbrook, 1991). For discussions of feminist pedagogy in composition, see, for instance, Susan Hunter (1991) and Susan Osborn (1991), as well as the essays collected by Cynthia Caywood and Gillian Overing (1987).

17. The openness of the exploratory or personal essay shouldn't be overstated, however. The personal essay is a genre in its own right, with its own conventions and history (Hesse, 1991). My reason for discussing it here is not that it is an entirely free or open form, but that it offers a clear alternative to conventional academic genres such as the empirical report.

18. The general term *literary nonfiction* applies to the type of science essay Comprone discusses, as well as to other types of writing in which factual accuracy and evocative power are both valued. For a discussion of this point with a well-known writer of literary nonfiction—John McPhee—see Douglas Vipond and Russell Hunt (1991); for a more general discussion of the genre, see the essays collected by Chris Anderson (1989).

19. For more discussion of the place of narrative in psychology, see, for instance, Jerome Bruner (1986, chap. 2), Donald Polkinghorne (1988, chap. 5), Theodore Sarbin (1986), Donald Spence (1982), and Paul Vitz (1990).

CHAPTER 4

1. In Kenneth Burke's (1966) terms, handbooks provide a set of "terministic screens" that simultaneously direct and deflect attention: "Even if any given terminology is a *reflection* of reality, by its very nature as a terminology it must be a *selection* of reality; and to this extent it must function also as a *deflection* of reality" (p. 45). For a different view of "definite, specific, concrete," based on the pedagogy of Ira Shor (1980), see Virginia Perdue (1990). Perdue suggests that details can be catalysts for changing students' consciousness.

2. The exercises have now been published separately; see Harold Gelfand and Charles Walker (1990).

3. For a sustained critique of current-traditional rhetoric and handbooks, see Sharon Crowley (1990, chap. 8). Crowley might describe the *Manual* as a "*very*-current-traditional" handbook. The term *current-traditional* is discussed in Chapter 1, note 7.

4. The point is made by Bazerman, who writes,

Only when a community decides there is one right way, can it gain the confidence and narrowness of detailed prescriptions. In rhetoric, "one right way" implies not only a stability of text, but a stability of rhetorical situation, roles, relations, and actions, so that there is little room or motive for improvisatory argument. Within a stabilized rhetorical universe, people will want to say similar things to each other under similar conditions for similar purposes. (Bazerman, 1988, p. 271)

5. The IMRAD format is widely but not universally used in the sciences. Journals such as *Science, Nature, Physical Review,* and *Behavioral and Brain Sciences* all use ad-hoc headings, not IMRAD.

6. According to Robert Day (1988), the IMRAD format is so "eminently logical" that it can be used for many kinds of expository writing. "Whether one is writing an article about chemistry, archeology, economics, or crime in the streets, the IMRAD format is often the best choice," he says (p. 11). Day doesn't consider, however, that the terministic screen *logical* may be deflecting attention from other realities.

7. Similarly, Karl Popper (1963) contrasts an accumulative with a language-based view of science, opting for the latter.

It is necessary for us to see that of the two main ways in which we may explain the growth of science, one is rather unimportant and the other is important. The first explains science by the accumulation of knowledge: it is like a growing library (or a museum). As more and more books accumulate, so more and more knowledge accumulates. The other explains it by criticism: it grows by a more revolutionary method than accumulation—by a method which destroys, changes, and alters the whole thing, including its most important instrument, the language in which our myths and theories are formulated. (Popper, 1963, p. 129)

8. By "shackling" every item to a particular point in time (Stringer, 1990, p. 28), the author–date or Harvard system has trouble with posthumously published work, producing what appear to be historical bloopers: "Freud, 1953," "Aristotle, 1987," "Erasmus, 1978." Unlike the APA system, MLA (Modern Language Association) style—widely used in rhetoric and composition studies—foregrounds names, but not dates; writers do not have to commit themselves to a particular date for each citation (Gibaldi and Achtert). For a discussion of the persuasive value of citing and referencing, see G. Nigel Gilbert (1977).

9. Unless indicated otherwise, all subsequent references will be to this edition.

10. George Orwell's (1946/1968a) rule was, "If it is possible to cut a word out, always cut it out" (p. 139). Strunk and White (1979) are even more concise: "Omit needless words" (p. 23).

11. There was a pedagogical point to such abundance, however, as Corbett explains:

By artificially experimenting with various forms, students became aware of the flexibility of the language in which they were working and learned to extend their own range. Ultimately they learned that although there is a variety of ways of saying something, there is a "best way" for their particular subject matter, occasion, or audience. What was "best" for one occasion or audience, they discovered, is not "best" for another occasion or audience. (Corbett, 1990, p. 462)

12. According to James Zappen (1989), Bacon was not a plain stylist pure and simple. Rather, he advocated different styles for different parts of his scientific method. Although he recommended plain style for the writing of natural and experimental history, for the more advanced and specialized inductive work Bacon favored an "imaginative" style.

13. In Book III of *Gulliver's Travels*, Jonathan Swift (1735/1962) satirized this notion: If *words* and *things* are equivalent, why not carry around with us all the *things* necessary for expression, thereby saving our lungs from needless wear and tear? Swift says that many of the most learned and wise men (Royal Society members)—adopting this new way of expression—carry the *things* they wish to talk about on their backs. When two such men meet in the street they "lay down their loads, open their sacks and hold conversation for an hour together; then put up their implements, help each other to resume their burthens, and take their leave" (p. 184).

14. As discussed in Chapter 2, it's doubtful whether "the reader" can be so easily characterized, however. Bazerman's (1985) study of physicists' professional reading suggests that scientists read for many different purposes. Sometimes, in "self-tutorial" mode, they may read quite uncritically, in order to fill in background knowledge; at other times, when reading an article directly relevant to their own research, they may read extremely critically and skeptically. Far from looking for *the* theme, theoreticians and experimentalists may be interested in different types of information due to their different purposes and knowledge. Reader-response theory, as well, teaches us to be wary of any claim that all readers or readings are alike (Rosenblatt, 1978; Vipond & Hunt, 1984).

15. To the best of my knowledge, George Orwell (1946/1968b) was the first to use the window metaphor, in 1946. "One can write nothing readable unless one constantly struggles to efface one's own personality," Orwell said. "Good prose is like a window pane" (p. 7).

16. One difficulty with such an anti-rhetoric rhetoric is that it makes the teaching and learning of writing extremely difficult, because "it is hard to teach and learn what, it being transparent, you cannot see" (Lanham, 1983, p. 95).

17. Similarly, readers should be able to look right through texts without being distracted by the *writer* in the text. Edwin G. Boring (1957), then editor of *Contemporary Psychology*, recommended that writers of psychology refer to themselves in such a way that they become transparent: "The only rule, *CP* thinks, is for the writer to write so that the reader will not notice what the writer does in this respect." Boring would agree with Orwell (see note 15, above) that a writer should "efface one's own personality." Thus the often remarked "impersonality" of scientific writing may be due in part to writers' and editors' allegiance to the windowpane notion of clarity.

18. Canadian readers will recognize the related C-B-C theory in which "clarity," "brevity," and "correctness" are dominant.

19. The assumption that reading is a "burden" is interesting: Could the *Manual* be an expression of the Protestant ethic? The third edition says, "By developing ideas clearly and logically, you invite readers to read . . . and make their task agreeable by leading them smoothly from thought to thought" (American Psychological Association, 1983, p. 31). The implication is not only that readers are passive, but that their "task" wasn't very agreeable in the first place. Elsewhere the *Manual* describes writing for publication as "sometimes tedious" (p. 17). Compare these lugubrious assumptions with poststructural and deconstructionist thought (for example, Barthes, 1973/1975), in which writing and reading are conceived as playful, pleasurable activities—the joy of texts, as it were.

20. I find Laib's work valuable because it addresses a tension in writing as a social act. From one perspective, writing can be seen as helpful, teacherly, prosocial; from another, it is an imposition, authoritarian (Clark, 1990, chap. 4), an act of territoriality (Laib, 1985). If advancing knowledge claims is, as Greg Myers (1989) suggests, inherently impolite, then concise writing could be one

way of mitigating the impoliteness. Paradoxically, though, too much concision can result in bluntness—which is also impolite.

CHAPTER 5

1. Or, as the developmental psychologist George Butterworth (1981) once said, explaining his interest in infants' conceptions of causality, "Not all babies become philosophers, but all philosophers were once babies."

2. I limit the discussion to undergraduate psychology teaching because I don't feel qualified to comment on graduate courses. Presumably, though, many of the suggestions made for undergraduates would apply, with appropriate adjustments, to the graduate level.

3. Thus there tends to be a tension between teaching composition and teaching in the "content" disciplines. Correspondingly, there is much debate concerning the *politics* of writing instruction: What purposes does it serve? Who is it for? Who pays for it? James Slevin writes,

The politics of teaching writing is about the most important issues now confronting higher education: it is about the kinds of students who get to attend and to succeed at the college and university, about the authenticity of our commitment to democratic education; it is about what happens to them there and how their writing can make a difference for them; and it is about our understanding of what it means to know and change what is claimed to be known. (Slevin, 1991, p. 154)

4. For an examination of commercial interests and other aspects of the political economy of textbook publishing, see Michael Apple (1986, chap. 4). Apple's article is reprinted in Suzanne de Castell, Allan Luke, and Carmen Luke (1989), which contains many other interesting studies as well. A classic study of bias in social studies texts is that of Frances FitzGerald (1979); Diane B. Paul (1987) and Harriet Tyson-Bernstein (1988) provide useful overviews. *Teaching of Psychology* often publishes articles of the type "The Inadequate Treatment of *X* in Psychology Textbooks," and occasionally more general discussions such as that of Wilbert McKeachie (1976). Peter Stringer (1990) and Jill Morawski (1992) take a more analytic approach. Robert Boynton (1988) and Hans Guth, Robert Boynton, and James Squire (1989) discuss textbooks in English and composition.

5. One criticism of short-answer testing is that it tends to confuse "knowledge" and "information." As Kurt Danziger (1990c) notes, this confusion is implicit in the Baconian approach to science, where science is seen as information gathering: The more bits or facts you have collected, the more knowledge you have. But more important than the accumulation of facts is the *construction of knowledge*; what ultimately counts is not mass of information, but "broad theoretical relevance and fertile cognitive texture" (p. 277). Psychology has plenty of information, Danziger writes, but "too little of it is rich in the qualities of knowledge that is not just a compendium" (p. 277). As anyone who has tried

to construct a multiple-choice test can verify, it is extremely difficult to write items that imply anything other than a compendium.

6. Discussions and examples of WAC can be found in Toby Fulwiler and Art Young (1990), Anne Herrington and Charles Moran (1992), Susan McLeod (1988), Barbara Walvoord and Lucille McCarthy (1990), and Art Young and Toby Fulwiler (1986). For a historical perspective, see David Russell (1991).

7. For further discussion of freewriting, see the volume edited by Pat Belanoff, Peter Elbow, and Sheryl Fontaine (1991); for more on journals, see Toby Fulwiler (1987a).

8. James Moffett writes,

For the teacher to act as audience is a very intricate matter fraught with hazards that need special attention. . . . [The teacher] is at once parental substitute, civic authority, and the wielder of marks. Any one of these roles would be potent enough to distort the writer–audience relationship; all together, they cause the student to misuse the feedback in ways that severely limit [the student's] learning to write. (Moffett, 1968, p. 193)

As Russell Hunt (1987) suggests, there is a large difference between responding to a student's formal and mechanical errors and responding to the student's meaning; in Randall Jarrell's fable "The Bat-Poet," this is the difference between the analytic response of the mockingbird and the engaged response of the chipmunk. For further discussion, see C. H. Knoblauch and Lil Brannon (1984, chap. 6) and Nancy Sommers (1982).

9. Implications of computers for the teaching of writing are discussed by Marilyn Cooper and Cynthia Selfe (1990), Lester Faigley (1992, chap. 6), Gail Hawisher and Cynthia Selfe (1989), Selfe (1989), and William Wresch (1991). Also relevant is the journal, *Computers and Composition*, edited by Hawisher and Selfe. For applications in psychology, see, for instance, Arnold Kahn and Robert Brookshire (1991) and Sara Kiesler, Jane Siegel, and Timothy McGuire (1984).

10. For further discussion of collaborative learning and the teaching of writing, see, for instance, Lisa Ede and Andrea Lunsford (1990, chap. 4), Peter Elbow (1973), Richard Gebhardt (1980), and Anne Herrington and Deborah Cadman (1991). Ann Ruggles Gere (1987) provides a historical perspective.

11. Further discussion and examples of "collaborative investigation" are provided by James Reither (1990) and Art Young (1990).

12. Portfolio evaluation is rapidly becoming the method of choice in writing classrooms and programs; for discussion, see Pat Belanoff and Marcia Dickson (1991) and Marjorie Roemer, Lucille Schultz, and Russel Durst (1991).

13. Ideas about such community publishing projects are presented by Jan Fluitt-Dupuy (1989) and Keith Kimberley (1989). Kimberley defends autobiographical texts because they "den[y] to teacher and school textbook the status of sole sources of authority. . . . Where there is regular use of alternative, and sometimes therefore awkward or oppositional, texts alongside those which dominate the mainstream curriculum, some of the conditions are established for real learning" (p. 193).

14. See Karen Howe (1989) for a description of women students who wrote biographies of their mothers. Howe suggests that the students thereby increased their understanding both of their mothers and themselves.

15. Kieran Egan (1989) argues for the storied basis of science and encourages science teachers to incorporate mythic stories in their teaching. For discussions of the place of narrative in psychology, see the references cited in Chapter 3, note 19, above.

References

American Psychiatric Association. (1987). *Diagnostic and statistical manual of mental disorders* (3rd ed. rev.). Washington: Author.

American Psychological Association. (1974). *Publication manual of the American Psychological Association* (2nd ed.). Washington: Author.

American Psychological Association. (1983). *Publication manual of the American Psychological Association* (3rd ed.). Washington: Author.

American Psychological Association Council of Editors. (1952). Publication manual of the American Psychological Association. *Psychological Bulletin, 49* [Supplement], 389–449.

Anderson, Chris. (1988). Hearsay evidence and second-class citizenship. *College English, 50*, 300–308.

Anderson, Chris (Ed.). (1989). *Literary nonfiction: Theory, criticism, pedagogy.* Carbondale and Edwardsville: Southern Illinois University Press.

Anderson, John E., & Valentine, Willard L. (1944). The preparation of articles for publication in the journals of the American Psychological Association. *Psychological Bulletin, 41*, 345–376.

Apple, Michael W. (1986). *Teachers and texts: A political economy of class and gender relations in education.* New York and London: Routledge & Kegan Paul.

Arrington, Phillip. (1991). The agon over what "composition research" means. *Journal of Advanced Composition, 11*, 377–393.

Arrington, Phillip, & Farmer, Frank. (1989). [Review of Barbara E. Walvoord's *Three steps to revising your writing for style, grammar, punctuation, and spelling*, Joseph M. Williams's *Style: Ten lessons in clarity and grace*, and William Vande Kopple's *Clear and coherent prose: A func-*

tional approach]. *College Composition and Communication, 40*, 486–489.

Bain, Alexander. (1866). *English composition and rhetoric: A manual*. London: Longmans.

Bakhtin, Mikhail M. (1981). Discourse in the novel. In *The dialogic imagination* (Michael Holquist, Ed.; Caryl Emerson & Michael Holquist, Trans.). Austin: University of Texas Press. (Original work published 1935)

Barthes, Roland. (1975). *The pleasure of the text* (Richard Miller, Trans.). New York: Hill and Wang. (Original work published 1973)

Bartholomae, David. (1985). Inventing the university. In Mike Rose (Ed.), *When a writer can't write: Studies in writer's block and other composing-process problems* (pp. 134–165). New York: Guilford.

Bartholomae, David. (1989). Freshman English, composition, and CCCC. *College Composition and Communication, 40*, 38–50.

Bazerman, Charles. (1985). Physicists reading physics: Schema-laden purposes and purpose-laden schema. *Written Communication, 2*, 3–23.

Bazerman, Charles. (1988). *Shaping written knowledge: The genre and activity of the experimental article in science*. Madison: University of Wisconsin Press.

Bazerman, Charles, & Paradis, James (Eds.). (1991). *Textual dynamics of the professions: Historical and contemporary studies of writing in professional communities*. Madison: University of Wisconsin Press.

Beers, Susan E. (1985). Use of a portfolio writing assignment in a course on developmental psychology. *Teaching of Psychology, 12*, 94–96.

Belanoff, Pat, & Dickson, Marcia (Eds.). (1991). *Portfolios: Process and product*. Portsmouth, NH: Boynton/Cook.

Belanoff, Pat, Elbow, Peter, & Fontaine, Sheryl I. (Eds.). (1991). *Nothing begins with N: New investigations of freewriting*. Carbondale and Edwardsville: Southern Illinois University Press.

Belenky, Mary Field, Clinchy, Blythe McVicker, Goldberger, Nancy Rule, & Tarule, Jill Mattuck. (1986). *Women's ways of knowing: The development of self, voice, and mind*. New York: Basic Books.

Bem, Daryl J. (1987). Writing the empirical journal article. In Mark P. Zanna & John M. Darley (Eds.), *The compleat academic: A practical guide for the beginning social scientist* (pp. 171–201). New York: Random House.

Benjamin, Ludy T., Jr. (1991). Personalization and active learning in the large introductory psychology class. *Teaching of Psychology, 18*, 68–74.

Bentley, Madison, Peerenboom, C. A., Hodge, F. W., Passano, Edward B., Warren, H. C., & Washburn, M. F. (1929). Instructions in regard to preparation of manuscript. *Psychological Bulletin, 26*, 57–63.

Berkenkotter, Carol. (1991). Paradigm debates, turf wars, and the conduct of sociocognitive inquiry in composition. *College Composition and Communication, 42*, 151–169.

References

e, Robert. (1987b). Underlife and writing instruction. *College Composition and Communication, 38*, 141–153.

e, Kenneth A. (1983). Writing and reading as collaborative or social acts. In Janice N. Hays, Phyllis A. Roth, Jon R. Ramsey, & Robert D. Foulke (Eds.), *The writer's mind: Writing as a mode of thinking* (pp. 159–169). Urbana, IL: National Council of Teachers of English.

, Kenneth A. (1984). Collaborative learning and "the conversation of mankind." *College English, 46*, 635–642.

, Jerome S. (1960). *The process of education.* Cambridge, MA: Harvard University Press.

, Jerome S. (1962). *On knowing: Essays for the left hand.* Cambridge, MA: Harvard University Press.

, Jerome. (1986). *Actual minds, possible worlds.* Cambridge, MA: Harvard University Press.

, Jerome, & Feldman, Carol Fleisher. (1990). Metaphors of consciousness and cognition in the history of psychology. In David E. Leary (Ed.), *Metaphors in the history of psychology* (pp. 230–238). Cambridge, England: Cambridge University Press.

, Louis C., & Nichols, Julia A. (1981). Citation impact, acceptance rate, and APA journals. *American Psychologist, 36*, 1453–1456.

is, Peter, & Coe, Richard M. (Eds.). (1988). Canadian literature and rhetoric [Special issue]. *College English, 50*(8).

Chris J. (1990). Changing the context: Applying feminist perspectives to the writing class. *English Quarterly, 22*(3/4), 141–148.

Richard, Trimbur, John, & Schuster, Charles (Eds). (1991). *The politics of writing instruction: Postsecondary.* Portsmouth, NH: Boynton.

enneth. (1950). Rhetoric—old and new. *Journal of General Education, , 202–209.

enneth. (1966). *Language as symbolic action: Essays on life, literature, nd method.* Berkeley: University of California Press.

enneth. (1969). *A rhetoric of motives.* Berkeley and Los Angeles: University of California Press. (Original work published 1950)

enneth. (1973). *The philosophy of literary form: Studies in symbolic ction* (3rd ed.). Berkeley: University of California Press.

rth, George. (1981). Paper presented to the Psychology Department, niversity of New Brunswick, Fredericton, New Brunswick, Canda.

s here are growth, excitement. (1992, September). *APA Monitor*, pp.)–51.

izanne de, Luke, Allan, & Luke, Carmen (Eds.). (1989). *Language, thority and criticism: Readings on the school textbook.* London: lmer Press.

ary Kupiec. (1990). What happens when things go wrong: Women d writing blocks. *Journal of Advanced Composition, 10*, 321–338.

Berlin, James A. (1987). *Rhetoric and reality: Writ colleges, 1900–1985*. Carbondale and Edv University Press.

Berthoff, Ann E. (1971). The problem of problem s *and Communication, 22*, 237–242.

Bettelheim, Bruno. (1984). *Freud and man's soul.*

Billig, Michael. (1987). *Arguing and thinking: A psychology*. Cambridge, England: Cambri

Billig, Michael. (1990). Rhetoric of social psych Shotter (Eds.), *Deconstructing social psy* and New York: Routledge.

Billig, Michael. (1991). *Ideology and opinions: ogy*. London: Sage.

Bizzell, Patricia. (1982). Cognition, convention, know about writing. *PRE/TEXT, 3*, 213–

Bizzell, Patricia, & Herzberg, Bruce. (1990). *The from classical times to the present.* B Martin's Press.

Bleich, David. (1989). Genders of writing. *Jour* 10–25.

Bleich, David. (1990). Sexism in academic st *vanced Composition, 10*, 231–247.

Bohan, Janis S. (1990). Social constructioni expanded approach to the history of p *ogy, 17*, 82–89.

Bond, Lynne A., & Magistrale, Anthony S. (19 Lexington, MA: D. C. Heath.

Boring, Edwin G. (1957). *CP speaks . . . Cont*

Boynton, Robert. (1988). Somewhere over the classes. *English Education, 20*, 206–2

Braddock, Richard, Lloyd-Jones, Richard, & *in written composition*. Champaign, I English. (ERIC Document Reproduc

Brand, Alice Glarden. (1980). *Therapy in wr prise*. Lexington, MA: D. C. Heath.

Brand, Alice Glarden. (1989). *The psycholo ence*. New York: Greenwood Press.

Bridwell-Bowles, Lillian. (1991). Research i In Erika Lindemann & Gary Tate (E *studies* (pp. 94–117). New York: O

Britton, James, Burgess, Tony, Martin, Nan (1975). *The development of writing* land: Macmillan Education.

Brooke, Robert. (1987a). Lacan, transfere *English, 49*, 679–691.

Brook

Bruffe

Bruffe

Bruner

Bruner

Bruner

Bruner,

Buffard

Buitenh

Bullock,

Bullock,

Burke, K

Burke, K

Burke, K

Burke, K

Butterwo

Buzzword

Castell, S

Cayton, M

Caywood, Cynthia L., & Overing, Gillian R. (Eds.). (1987). *Teaching writing: Pedagogy, gender, and equity*. Albany: State University of New York Press.

Chamberlain, Kerry, & Burrough, Stephen. (1985). Techniques for teaching critical reading. *Teaching of Psychology, 12*, 213–215.

Chappell, Virginia A. (1991). Teaching like a reader instead of reading like a teacher. In Virginia A. Chappell, Mary Louise Buley-Meissner, & Chris Anderson (Eds.), *Balancing acts: Essays on the teaching of writing in honor of William F. Irmscher* (pp. 53–66). Carbondale and Edwardsville: Southern Illinois University Press.

Charlesworth, John R., Jr., & Slate, John R. (1986). Teaching about puberty: Learning to talk about sensitive topics. *Teaching of Psychology, 13*, 215–217.

Clark, Gregory. (1990). *Dialogue, dialectic, and conversation: A social perspective on the function of writing*. Carbondale and Edwardsville: Southern Illinois University Press.

Clifford, John. (1991). Toward a productive crisis: A response to Gayatri Spivak. *Journal of Advanced Composition, 11*, 191–196.

Coe, Richard M. (1987). An apology for form; or, who took the form out of the process? *College English, 49*, 13–28.

Coe, Rick. (1993). What is inkshedding? *Inkshed: Newsletter of the Canadian Association for the Study of Writing and Reading, 11*(3), 1–3.

Cohen, Ronald Jay, Montague, Pamela, Nathanson, Linda Sue, & Swerdlik, Mark E. (1992a). An inappropriate reviewer? *Contemporary Psychology, 37*, 504.

Cohen, Ronald Jay, Montague, Pamela, Nathanson, Linda Sue, & Swerdlik, Mark E. (1992b). The only one hurting Valencia is Valencia. *Contemporary Psychology, 37*, 505.

Comprone, Joseph J. (1989). Narrative topic and the contemporary science essay: A lesson from Loren Eiseley's notebooks. *Journal of Advanced Composition, 9*, 112–123.

Conference on College Composition and Communication. (1989). Statement of principles and standards for the postsecondary teaching of writing. *College Composition and Communication, 40*, 329–336.

Connors, Robert J. (1983a). Composition studies and science. *College English, 45*, 1–20.

Connors, Robert J. (1983b). Handbooks: History of a genre. *Rhetoric Society Quarterly, 13*, 87–98.

Connors, Robert J. (1984). Journals in composition studies. *College English, 46*, 348–365.

Connors, Robert J. (1991). Writing the history of our discipline. In Erika Lindemann & Gary Tate (Eds.), *An introduction to composition studies* (pp. 49–71). New York: Oxford University Press.

Cooper, Marilyn M. (1986). The ecology of writing. *College English, 48*, 364–375.

Cooper, Marilyn M. (1989). Why are we talking about discourse communities? Or, foundationalism rears its ugly head once more. In Marilyn M. Cooper & Michael Holzman, *Writing as social action* (pp. 202–220). Portsmouth, NH: Boynton/Cook.

Cooper, Marilyn M., & Selfe, Cynthia L. (1990). Computer conferences and learning: Authority, resistance, and internally persuasive discourse. *College English, 52,* 847–869.

Corbett, Edward P. J. (1990). *Classical rhetoric for the modern student* (3rd ed.). New York: Oxford University Press.

Crowley, Sharon. (1990). *The methodical memory: Invention in current-traditional rhetoric.* Carbondale and Edwardsville: Southern Illinois University Press.

Czubaroff, Jeanine. (1989). The deliberative character of strategic scientific debates. In Herbert W. Simons (Ed.), *Rhetoric in the human sciences* (pp. 28–47). London: Sage.

Daiker, Donald A., Kerek, Andrew, & Morenberg, Max. (1979). *The writer's options: College sentence combining.* New York: Harper & Row.

Daly, John A. (1985). Writing apprehension. In Mike Rose (Ed.), *When a writer can't write: Studies in writer's block and other composing-process problems* (pp. 43–82). New York: Guilford.

Danziger, Kurt. (1990a). *Constructing the subject: Historical origins of psychological research.* Cambridge, England: Cambridge University Press.

Danziger, Kurt. (1990b). Generative metaphor and the history of psychological discourse. In David E. Leary (Ed.), *Metaphors in the history of psychology* (pp. 331–356). Cambridge, England: Cambridge University Press.

Danziger, Kurt. (1990c). Malthus for psychology? *Canadian Psychology, 31,* 276–278.

Day, Robert A. (1988). *How to write and publish a scientific paper* (3rd ed.). Phoenix, NY: Oryx Press.

Derrida, Jacques. (1976). *Of grammatology* (Gayatri C. Spivak, Trans.). Baltimore: Johns Hopkins University Press.

Dias, Patrick, Beer, Ann, Ledwell-Brown, Jane, Paré, Anthony, & Pittenger, Carolyn. (1992). *Writing for ourselves/writing for others.* Scarborough, ON: Nelson Canada.

Dixon, John. (1967). *Growth through English: A report based on the Dartmouth Seminar, 1966.* Reading, England: National Association for the Teaching of English.

Ede, Lisa, & Lunsford, Andrea. (1984). Audience addressed/audience invoked: The role of audience in composition theory and pedagogy. *College Composition and Communication, 35,* 155–171.

Ede, Lisa, & Lunsford, Andrea. (1990). *Singular texts/plural authors: Perspectives on collaborative writing.* Carbondale and Edwardsville: Southern Illinois University Press.

Egan, Kieran. (1989). The shape of the science text: A function of stories. In Suzanne de Castell, Allan Luke, & Carmen Luke (Eds.), *Language, authority and criticism: Readings on the school textbook* (pp. 96–108). London: Falmer Press.

Elbow, Peter. (1973). *Writing without teachers*. London: Oxford University Press.

Elbow, Peter. (1987). Closing my eyes as I speak: An argument for ignoring audience. *College English, 49*, 50–69.

Elbow, Peter. (1990). Forward: About personal expressive academic writing. *PRE/TEXT, 11*(1/2), 7–20.

Elbow, Peter. (1991). Reflections on academic discourse: How it relates to freshmen and colleagues. *College English, 53*, 135–155.

Emig, Janet. (1971). *The composing processes of twelfth graders*. Urbana, IL: National Council of Teachers of English.

Emig, Janet. (1977). Writing as a mode of learning. *College Composition and Communication, 28*, 122–128.

Erasmus, Desiderius. (1978). *Collected works of Erasmus: Vol. 2. Literary and educational writings* (Craig R. Thompson, Ed.). Toronto: University of Toronto Press. (Original work published 1512)

Estrin, Herman A. (1981). Engineering students write books for children. In Dwight W. Stevenson (Ed.), *Courses, components, and exercises in technical communication* (pp. 132–135). Urbana, IL: National Council of Teachers of English.

Ewald, Helen Rothschild. (1991). What we could tell advanced student writers about audience. *Journal of Advanced Composition, 11*, 147–158.

Fahnestock, Jeanne. (1986). Accommodating science: The rhetorical life of scientific facts. *Written Communication, 3*, 275–296.

Fahnestock, Jeanne. (1991). Teaching argumentation in the junior-level course. In Katherine H. Adams & John L. Adams (Eds.), *Teaching advanced composition: Why and how* (pp. 179–193). Portsmouth, NH: Boynton/Cook.

Faigley, Lester. (1986). Competing theories of process: A critique and a proposal. *College English, 48*, 527–542.

Faigley, Lester. (1992). *Fragments of rationality: Postmodernity and the subject of composition*. Pittsburgh, PA, and London: University of Pittsburgh Press.

Feingold, Alan. (1989). Assessment of journals in social science psychology. *American Psychologist, 44*, 961–964.

Fine, Michelle. (1989). Coping with rape: Critical perspectives on consciousness. In Rhoda K. Unger (Ed.), *Representations: Social constructions of gender* (pp. 186–200). Amityville, NY: Baywood.

FitzGerald, Frances. (1979). *America revised: History schoolbooks in the twentieth century*. Boston: Little, Brown.

Flower, Linda. (1981). *Problem-solving strategies for writing*. New York: Harcourt Brace Jovanovich.

Flower, Linda S., & Hayes, John R. (1977). Problem-solving strategies and the writing process. *College English, 39*, 449–461.

Fluitt-Dupuy, Jan. (1989). Publishing a newsletter: Making composition classes more meaningful. *College Composition and Communication, 40*, 219–223.

Flynn, Elizabeth A. (1988). Composing as a woman. *College Composition and Communication, 39*, 423–435.

Fogarty, Daniel. (1959). *Roots for a new rhetoric*. New York: Teachers College Press.

Foss, Donald J. (1985). *CP* speaks. *Contemporary Psychology, 30*, 933–935.

Freire, Paulo. (1970). *Pedagogy of the oppressed* (Myra Bergman Ramos, Trans.). New York: Continuum.

Frey, Olivia. (1990). Beyond literary Darwinism: Women's voices and critical discourse. *College English, 52*, 507–526.

Fulwiler, Toby (Ed.). (1987a). *The journal book*. Portsmouth, NH: Boynton/Cook.

Fulwiler, Toby. (1987b). Using a journal. In Lynne A. Bond & Anthony S. Magistrale, *Writer's guide: Psychology* (pp. 19–32). Lexington, MA: D. C. Heath.

Fulwiler, Toby, & Young, Art (Eds.). (1990). *Programs that work: Models and methods for writing across the curriculum*. Portsmouth, NH: Boynton/Cook.

Furumoto, Laurel. (1988). Shared knowledge: The experimentalists, 1904–1929. In Jill G. Morawski (Ed.), *The rise of experimentation in American psychology* (pp. 94–113). New Haven, CT, and London: Yale University Press.

Gage, John T. (1981). Towards an epistemology of composition. *Journal of Advanced Composition, 2*, 1–10.

Gage, John T. (1984). An adequate epistemology for composition: Classical and modern perspectives. In Robert J. Connors, Lisa S. Ede, & Andrea A. Lunsford (Eds.), *Essays on classical rhetoric and modern discourse* (pp. 152–169). Carbondale and Edwardsville: Southern Illinois University Press.

Gage, John T. (1991). On "rhetoric" and "composition." In Erika Lindemann & Gary Tate (Eds.), *An introduction to composition studies* (pp. 15–32). New York: Oxford University Press.

Gebhardt, Richard. (1980). Teamwork and feedback: Broadening the base of collaborative writing. *College English, 42*, 69–74.

Geertz, Clifford. (1983). *Local knowledge: Further essays in interpretive anthropology*. New York: Basic Books.

Gelfand, Harold, & Walker, Charles J. (1990). *Mastering APA style: Student's workbook and training guide*. Washington: American Psychological Association.

Gere, Anne Ruggles. (1987). *Writing groups: History, theory, and implications*. Carbondale and Edwardsville: Southern Illinois University Press.

Gibaldi, Joseph, & Achtert, Walter S. (1988). *MLA handbook for writers of research papers* (3rd ed.). New York: Modern Language Association.

Gibson, Walker. (1950). Authors, speakers, readers, and mock readers. *College English, 11*, 265–269.

Gilbert, G. Nigel. (1977). Referencing as persuasion. *Social Studies of Science, 7*, 113–122.

Gilligan, Carol. (1982). *In a different voice: Psychological theory and women's development.* Cambridge, MA: Harvard University Press.

Gorman, Michael E., Gorman, Margaret E., & Young, Art. (1986). Poetic writing in psychology. In Art Young & Toby Fulwiler (Eds.), *Writing across the disciplines: Research into practice* (pp. 139–159). Upper Montclair, NJ: Boynton/Cook.

Gragson, Gay, & Selzer, Jack. (1990). Fictionalizing the readers of scholarly articles in biology. *Written Communication, 7*, 25–58.

Granick, Lois. (1989). Preface. *PsycBooks 1987. Vol 1: Experimental psychology: Basic and applied* (pp. ix–x). Arlington, VA: American Psychological Association.

Graves, Roger. (1991, March). Composition studies in Canada, 1950–1990. Paper presented at the meetings of the Conference on College Composition and Communication, Boston.

Guth, Hans P., Boynton, Robert, & Squire, James R. (1989). The textbook gap. *English Journal, 78*(6), 13–21.

Hairston, Maxine. (1982). The winds of change: Thomas Kuhn and the revolution in the teaching of writing. *College Composition and Communication, 33*, 76–88.

Hairston, Maxine. (1990). [Comment]. *College English, 52*, 694–696.

Hairston, Maxine. (1992). Diversity, ideology, and teaching writing. *College Composition and Communication, 43*, 179–193.

Hall, G. Stanley. (1895). Editorial. *American Journal of Psychology, 7*, 3–8.

Halloran, S. Michael. (1990). From rhetoric to composition: The teaching of writing in America to 1900. In James J. Murphy (Ed.), *A short history of writing instruction: From ancient Greece to twentieth-century America* (pp. 151–182). Davis, CA: Hermagoras Press.

Halloran, S. Michael, & Bradford, Annette Norris. (1984). Figures of speech in the rhetoric of science and technology. In Robert J. Connors, Lisa S. Ede, & Andrea A. Lunsford (Eds.), *Essays on classical rhetoric and modern discourse* (pp. 179–192). Carbondale: Southern Illinois University Press.

Halloran, S. Michael, & Whitburn, Merrill D. (1982). Ciceronian rhetoric and the rise of science: The plain style reconsidered. In James J. Murphy (Ed.), *The rhetorical tradition and modern writing* (pp. 58–72). New York: Modern Language Association.

Harding, Sandra. (1986). *The science question in feminism.* Ithaca, NY, and London: Cornell University Press.

Harris, Joseph. (1989). The idea of community in the study of writing. *College Composition and Communication, 40*, 11–22.

Harris, Joseph. (1991). After Dartmouth: Growth and conflict in English. *College English, 53*, 631–646.

Harvey, John H. (1992). *CP* speaks. *Contemporary Psychology, 37*, 5–6.

Harvey, John H. (1993). *CP* speaks. *Contemporary Psychology, 38*, 7.

Hawisher, Gail E., & Selfe, Cynthia L. (Eds.). (1989). *Critical perspectives on computers and composition instruction*. New York and London: Teachers College Press.

Hawisher, Gail E., & Selfe, Cynthia L. (1991). The rhetoric of technology and the electronic writing class. *College Composition and Communication, 42*, 55–65.

Hayes, John R. (1992). A psychological perspective applied to literacy studies. In Richard Beach, Judith Green, Michael Kamil, & Timothy Shanahan (Eds.), *Multidisciplinary perspectives on literacy research* (pp. 125–139). Urbana, IL: National Conference on Research in English.

Hayes, John R., & Flower, Linda S. (1980). Identifying the organization of writing processes. In Lee W. Gregg & Erwin R. Steinberg (Eds.), *Cognitive processes in writing* (pp. 3–30). Hillsdale, NJ: Erlbaum.

Hebb, Donald O. (1980). D. O. Hebb. In Gardner Lindzey (Ed.), *A history of psychology in autobiography* (Vol. 7, pp. 273–303). San Francisco: W. H. Freeman.

Heider, Fritz. (1970). Gestalt theory: Early history and reminiscences. *Journal of the History of the Behavioral Sciences, 6*, 131–139.

Herrington, Anne J. (1992, March). Writing their way/writing mine: Writing for a psychology methods course. Paper presented at the meetings of the Conference on College Composition and Communication, Cincinnati.

Herrington, Anne J., & Cadman, Deborah. (1991). Peer review and revising in an anthropology course: Lessons for learning. *College Composition and Communication, 42*, 184–199.

Herrington, Anne, & Moran, Charles (Eds.). (1992). *Writing, teaching, and learning in the disciplines*. New York: Modern Language Association.

Hesse, Douglas. (1991). The recent rise of literary nonfiction: A cautionary assay. *Journal of Advanced Composition, 11*, 323–333.

Hillman, James, & Boer, Charles. (1985). *Freud's own cookbook*. New York: Harper & Row.

Hillocks, George, Jr. (1986). *Research on written composition: New directions for teaching*. Urbana, IL: National Conference on Research in English.

Hoffman, Robert R. (1980). Metaphor in science. In Richard P. Honeck & Robert R. Hoffman (Eds.), *Cognition and figurative language* (pp. 323–423). Hillsdale, NJ: Erlbaum.

Hoffman, Robert R., Cochran, Edward L., & Nead, James M. (1990). Cognitive metaphors in experimental psychology. In David E. Leary (Ed.), *Metaphors in the history of psychology* (pp. 173–229). Cambridge, England: Cambridge University Press.

Holbrook, Sue Ellen. (1991). Women's work: The feminizing of composition. *Rhetoric Review, 9*, 201–229.

Howard, George S. (1989). *A tale of two stories: Excursions into a narrative approach to psychology*. Notre Dame, IN: Academic Publications.

Howe, Karen G. (1989). Telling our mother's story: Changing daughters' perceptions of their mothers in a women's studies course. In Rhoda K. Unger (Ed.), *Representations: Social constructions of gender* (pp. 45–60). Amityville, NY: Baywood.

Hunt, Russell A. (1987). "Could you put in lots of holes?" Modes of response to writing. *Language Arts, 64*, 229–232.

Hunter, Susan. (1991). A woman's place *is* in the composition classroom: Pedagogy, gender, and difference. *Rhetoric Review, 9*, 230–245.

Irmscher, William F. (1987). Finding a comfortable identity. *College Composition and Communication, 38*, 81–87.

Jenkins, James J. (1991). Teaching psychology in large classes: Research and personal experience. *Teaching of Psychology, 18*, 74–80.

Jensen, George H., & DiTiberio, John K. (1989). *Personality and the teaching of composition*. Norwood, NJ: Ablex.

Jolley, Janina M., & Mitchell, Mark L. (1990). Two psychologists' experiences with journals. *Teaching of Psychology, 17*, 40–41.

Kahn, Arnold S., & Brookshire, Robert G. (1991). Using a computer bulletin board in a social psychology course. *Teaching of Psychology, 18*, 245–249.

Keller, Evelyn Fox. (1982). Feminism and science. *Signs: Journal of Women in Culture and Society, 7*, 589–602.

Keller, Evelyn Fox. (1985). *Reflections on gender and science*. New Haven, CT, & London: Yale University Press.

Kiesler, Sara, Siegel, Jane, & McGuire, Timothy W. (1984). Social psychological aspects of computer-mediated communication. *American Psychologist, 39*, 1123–1134.

Kimberley, Keith. (1989). Community publishing. In Suzanne de Castell, Allan Luke, & Carmen Luke (Eds.), *Language, authority and criticism: Readings on the school textbook* (pp. 184–194). London: Falmer Press.

Kirby, Sandra L., & McKenna, Kate. (1989). *Experience research social change: Methods from the margins*. Toronto: Garamond Press.

Knoblauch, C. H., & Brannon, Lil. (1984). *Rhetorical traditions and the teaching of writing*. Upper Montclair, NJ: Boynton/Cook.

Knorr-Cetina, Karin D. (1981). *The manufacture of knowledge: An essay on the constructivist and contextual nature of science*. Oxford, England: Pergamon.

Koulack, David, & Keselman, H. J. (1975). Ratings of psychology journals by members of the American Psychological Association. *American Psychologist, 30*, 1049–1053.

Kraemer, Don. (1990). No exit: A play of literacy and gender. *Journal of Advanced Composition, 10*, 305–320.

Kroll, Barry M. (1978). Cognitive egocentrism and the problem of audience awareness in written discourse. *Research in the Teaching of English, 12*, 269–281.

Kroll, Barry M. (1984). Writing for readers: Three perspectives on audience. *College Composition and Communication, 35*, 172–185.

LaBarbera, Joseph D., & Blanchard, Donna. (1992). A valid approach? *Contemporary Psychology, 37*, 1106.

Laib, Nevin K. (1985). Territoriality in rhetoric. *College English, 47*, 579–593.

Laib, Nevin K. (1990). Conciseness and amplification. *College Composition and Communication, 41*, 443–459.

Lakoff, George. (1986). A figure of thought. *Metaphor and Symbolic Activity, 1*, 215–225.

Lakoff, George, & Johnson, Mark. (1980). *Metaphors we live by*. Chicago and London: University of Chicago Press.

Lanham, Richard A. (1974). *Style: An anti-textbook*. New Haven, CT, and London: Yale University Press.

Lanham, Richard A. (1983). *Literacy and the survival of humanism*. New Haven, CT, and London: Yale University Press.

Larsen, Elizabeth. (1986). The effect of technology on the composing process. *Rhetoric Society Quarterly, 16*, 43–58.

Larson, Richard L. (1968). Discovery through questioning: A plan for teaching rhetorical invention. *College English, 30*, 126–134.

Latour, Bruno. (1987). *Science in action: How to follow scientists and engineers through society*. Cambridge, MA: Harvard University Press.

Latour, Bruno, & Woolgar, Steve. (1986). *Laboratory life: The construction of scientific facts* (2nd ed.). Princeton, NJ: Princeton University Press.

Lauer, Janice. (1970). Heuristics and composition. *College Composition and Communication, 21*, 396–404.

Leary, David E. (Ed.) (1990). *Metaphors in the history of psychology*. Cambridge, MA: Cambridge University Press.

LeFevre, Karen Burke. (1987). *Invention as a social act*. Carbondale and Edwardsville: Southern Illinois University Press.

Lerner, Gerda. (1986). *The creation of patriarchy*. New York: Oxford University Press.

Light, Richard J. (1990). *The Harvard Assessment Seminars: Explorations with students and faculty about teaching, learning, and student life* (1st report). Cambridge, MA: Harvard University.

Lindemann, Erika, & Tate, Gary (Eds.). (1991). *An introduction to composition studies*. New York: Oxford University Press.

Long, Russell C. (1980). Writer–audience relationships: Analysis or invention? *College Composition and Communication, 31*, 221–226.

Luke, Carmen, Castell, Suzanne de, & Luke, Allan. (1983). Beyond criticism: The authority of the school text. *Curriculum Inquiry, 13*(2), 111–127.

Lunsford, Andrea A. (1980). The content of basic writers' essays. *College Composition and Communication, 31*, 278–290.

Lunsford, Andrea A. (1991). The nature of composition studies. In Erika Lindemann & Gary Tate (Eds.), *An introduction to composition studies* (pp. 3–14). New York: Oxford University Press.

Lykes, M. Brinton. (1989). Dialogue with Guatemalan Indian women: Critical perspectives on constructing collaborative research. In Rhoda K. Unger (Ed.), *Representations: Social constructions of gender* (pp. 167–185). Amityville, NY: Baywood.

MacDonald, Susan. (1993). Becoming editors. *English Quarterly, 25*(1), 14–18.

MacDonald, Susan Peck. (1987). Problem definition in academic writing. *College English, 49*, 315–331.

Madden, Peter, & Engdahl, Lloyd. (1973, June). The EMPTI guide to swollen prose: The Engdahl-Madden Psychological Terms Inventory (EMPTI). *Psychology Today*, p. 99.

Matalene, Carolyn B. (Ed.). (1989). *Worlds of writing: Teaching and learning in discourse communities of work*. New York: Random House.

Matson, Johnny L., Gouvier, William Drew, & Manikam, Ramasamy. (1989). Publication counts and scholastic productivity: Comment on Howard, Cole, and Maxwell. *American Psychologist, 44*, 737–739.

McCarthy, Lucille Parkinson. (1991). A psychiatrist using *DSM-III*: The influence of a charter document in psychiatry. In Charles Bazerman & James Paradis (Eds.), *Textual dynamics of the professions: Historical and contemporary studies of writing in professional communities* (pp. 358–378). Madison: University of Wisconsin Press.

McConnell, James V. (1961). Learning theory. *Worm Runner's Digest, 3*, 117–128. (Reprinted in Harvey A. Katz, Patricia Warrick, & Martin Harry Greenberg, Eds., *Introductory psychology through science fiction*, pp. 111–124. Chicago: Rand McNally, 1974)

McGovern, Thomas V., Furumoto, Laurel, Halpern, Diane F., Kimble, Gregory A., & McKeachie, Wilbert J. (1991). Liberal education, study in depth, and the arts and sciences major—psychology. *American Psychologist, 46*, 598–605.

McGovern, Thomas V., & Hogshead, Deborah L. (1990). Learning about writing, thinking about teaching. *Teaching of Psychology, 17*, 5–10.

McKeachie, Wilbert J. (1976). Textbooks: Problems of publishers and professors. *Teaching of Psychology, 3*, 29–30.

McLeod, Susan. (1987). Some thoughts about feelings: The affective domain and the writing process. *College Composition and Communication, 38*, 426–435.

McLeod, Susan H. (Ed.). (1988). *Strengthening programs for writing across the curriculum*. San Francisco: Jossey-Bass.

McReynolds, Paul. (1990). Motives and metaphors: A study in scientific creativity. In David E. Leary (Ed.), *Metaphors in the history of psychology* (pp. 133–172). Cambridge, England: Cambridge University Press.

Melton, Arthur W. (1962). Editorial. *Journal of Experimental Psychology, 64*, 553–557.

Miller, Carolyn R. (1979). A humanistic rationale for technical writing. *College English, 40*, 610–617.

Miller, Carolyn R. (1984). Genre as social action. *Quarterly Journal of Speech, 70*, 151–167.

Miller, Susan. (1991). *Textual carnivals: The politics of composition*. Carbondale and Edwardsville: Southern Illinois University Press.

Mindess, Harvey. (1975). Hail to the chiefs. *American Psychologist, 30*, 598–600.

Moffett, James. (1968). *Teaching the universe of discourse*. Boston: Houghton Mifflin.

Moffett, James. (1982). Writing, inner speech, and meditation. *College English, 44*, 231–246.

Moran, Charles. (1991). A life in the profession. In Erika Lindemann & Gary Tate (Eds.), *An introduction to composition studies* (pp. 160–182). New York: Oxford University Press.

Morawski, Jill G. (1982). Assessing psychology's moral heritage through our neglected utopias. *American Psychologist, 37*, 1082–1095.

Morawski, Jill G. (1990). Telling stories. [Review of George S. Howard's *A tale of two stories: Excursions into a narrative approach to psychology*]. *Contemporary Psychology, 35*, 465–466.

Morawski, Jill G. (1992). There is more to our history of giving: The place of introductory textbooks in American psychology. *American Psychologist, 47*, 161–169.

Moulton, Janice. (1983). A paradigm of philosophy: The adversary method. In Sandra Harding & Merrill B. Hintikka (Eds.), *Discovering reality: Feminist perspectives on epistemology, metaphysics, methodology, and philosophy of science* (pp. 149–164). Dordrecht, The Netherlands: D. Reidl.

Mulderig, Gerald P. (1982). Nineteenth-century psychology and the shaping of Alexander Bain's *English composition and rhetoric*. In James J. Murphy (Ed.), *The rhetorical tradition and modern writing* (pp. 95–104). New York: Modern Language Association.

Mullins, Nicholas C. (1973). *Theories and theory groups in contemporary American sociology*. New York: Harper & Row.

Murphy, Ann. (1989). Transference and resistance in the basic writing classroom: Problematics and praxis. *College Composition and Communication, 40*, 175–187.

Myers, Greg. (1989). The pragmatics of politeness in scientific articles. *Applied Linguistics, 10*, 1–35.

Myers, Greg. (1990). *Writing biology: Texts in the social construction of scientific knowledge*. Madison: University of Wisconsin Press.

Nadelman, Lorraine. (1990). Learning to think and write as an empirical psychologist: The laboratory course in developmental psychology. *Teaching of Psychology, 17*, 45–48.

Newell, Allen, & Simon, Herbert A. (1972). *Human problem solving*. Englewood Cliffs, NJ: Prentice-Hall.

Nisbett, Richard E. (1990). The anticreativity letters: Advice from a senior tempter to a junior tempter. *American Psychologist, 45*, 1078–1082.

Nodine, Barbara F. (1990). Psychologists teach writing [Special issue]. *Teaching of Psychology, 17*(1).

North, Stephen M. (1987). *The making of knowledge in composition: Portrait of an emerging field*. Portsmouth, NH: Boynton/Cook.

Northey, Margot, & Timney, Brian. (1986). *Making sense in psychology and the life sciences: A student's guide to writing and style*. Toronto: Oxford University Press.

Odell, Lee, & Goswami, Dixie (Eds.). (1985). *Writing in nonacademic settings*. New York and London: Guilford.

Ohmann, Richard. (1979). Use definite, specific, concrete language. *College English, 41*, 390–397.

Ong, Walter J. (1975). The writer's audience is always a fiction. *PMLA, 90*, 9–21.

Orwell, George. (1968a). Politics and the English language. In Sonia Orwell & Ian Angus (Eds.), *The collected essays, journalism and letters of George Orwell: Vol. 4. In front of your nose, 1945–1950* (pp. 127–140). London: Secker & Warburg. (Original work published 1946)

Orwell, George. (1968b). Why I write. In Sonia Orwell & Ian Angus (Eds.), *The collected essays, journalism and letters of George Orwell: Vol. 1. An age like this, 1920–1940* (pp. 1–7). London: Secker & Warburg. (Original work published 1946)

Osberg, Timothy M. (1991). Teaching current advances in psychology: Student and instructor advantages. *Teaching of Psychology, 18*, 41–42.

Osborn, Susan. (1991). "Revision/re-vision": A feminist writing class. *Rhetoric Review, 9*, 258–273.

Pallak, Michael S. (1981). Editorial policy of the *American Psychologist*. *American Psychologist, 36*, 1473–1474.

Paradis, James, Dobrin, David, & Miller, Richard. (1985). Writing at Exxon ITD: Notes on the writing environment of an R&D organization. In Lee Odell & Dixie Goswami (Eds.), *Writing in nonacademic settings* (pp. 281–307). New York and London: Guilford Press.

Paré, Anthony. (1991). Ushering "audience" out: From oration to conversation. *Textual Studies in Canada, 1*, 45–64.

Paré, Anthony. (1993). A response to Rick Coe. *Inkshed: Newsletter of the Canadian Association for the Study of Writing and Reading, 11*(3), 3–5.

Park, Douglas B. (1982). The meanings of "audience." *College English, 44*, 247–257.

Park, Douglas B. (1986). Analyzing audiences. *College Composition and Communication, 37*, 478–488.

Parker, Patricia. (1987). *Literary fat ladies: Rhetoric, gender, property*. London and New York: Methuen.

Paul, Diane B. (1987). The nine lives of discredited data. *The Sciences, 27*(3), 26–30.

Pennebaker, James W. (1991). Self-expressive writing: Implications for health, education, and welfare. In Pat Belanoff, Peter Elbow, & Sheryl I. Fontaine (Eds.), *Nothing begins with N: New investigations of freewriting* (pp. 157–170). Carbondale and Edwardsville: Southern Illinois University Press.

Perdue, Virginia. (1990). The politics of teaching detail. *Rhetoric Review, 8,* 280–288.

Perl, Sondra. (1979). The composing processes of unskilled college writers. *Research in the Teaching of English, 13,* 317–336.

Pfister, Fred R., & Petrick, Joanne F. (1980). A heuristic model for creating a writer's audience. *College Composition and Communication, 31,* 213–220.

Phelps, Louise Wetherbee. (1985). Dialectics of coherence: Toward an integrative theory. *College English, 47,* 12–29.

Pittenger, Carolyn. (1986). Acknowledging acknowledging. *Inkshed: Newsletter of the Canadian Association for the Study of Writing and Reading, 5*(6), 4–5.

Polkinghorne, Donald E. (1988). *Narrative knowing and the human sciences.* Albany: State University of New York Press.

Popper, Karl R. (1963). *Conjectures and refutations: The growth of scientific knowledge.* London: Routledge & Kegan Paul.

Porter, James E. (1986). Intertextuality and the discourse community. *Rhetoric Review, 5,* 37–47.

Prelli, Lawrence J. (1989). *A rhetoric of science: Inventing scientific discourse.* Columbia: University of South Carolina Press.

Progoff, Ira. (1975). *At a journal workshop.* New York: Dialogue House Library.

Reddy, Michael J. (1979). The conduit metaphor: A case of frame conflict in our language about language. In Andrew Ortony (Ed.), *Metaphor and thought* (pp. 284–324). Cambridge, England: Cambridge University Press.

Reither, James A. (1985). Writing and knowing: Toward redefining the writing process. *College English, 47,* 620–628.

Reither, James A. (1990). The writing *student* as researcher: Learning from our students. In Donald A. Daiker & Max Morenberg (Eds.), *The writing teacher as researcher: Essays in the theory and practice of class-based research* (pp. 247–255). Portsmouth, NH: Boynton/Cook.

Reither, James A. (1991, August). [Assistant chair position statement]. Conference on College Composition and Communication, Urbana, IL.

Reither, James A., & Vipond, Douglas. (1989). Writing as collaboration. *College English, 51,* 855–867.

Roemer, Marjorie, Schultz, Lucille M., & Durst, Russel K. (1991). Portfolios and the process of change. *College Composition and Communication, 42,* 455–469.

Rohman, D. Gordon. (1965). Pre-writing: The stage of discovery in the writing process. *College Composition and Communication, 16*, 106–112.

Rorty, Richard. (1979). *Philosophy and the mirror of nature*. Princeton, NJ: Princeton University Press.

Rose, Mike. (1990). *Lives on the boundary: A moving account of the struggles and achievements of America's educational underclass*. New York: Penguin.

Rosenblatt, Louise M. (1976). *Literature as exploration* (3rd ed.). New York: Barnes and Noble. (Original work published 1938)

Rosenblatt, Louise M. (1978). *The reader, the text, the poem: The transactional theory of the literary work*. Carbondale: Southern Illinois University Press.

Rosnow, Ralph L., & Rosnow, Mimi. (1986). *Writing papers in psychology: A student guide*. Belmont, CA: Wadsworth.

Roth, Geneen. (1982). *Feeding the hungry heart: The experience of compulsive eating*. Indianapolis, IN, and New York: Bobbs-Merrill.

Russell, David R. (1991). *Writing in the academic disciplines, 1870–1990: A curricular history*. Carbondale and Edwardsville: Southern Illinois University Press.

Sampson, Edward E. (1988). The debate on individualism: Indigenous psychologies of the individual and their role in personal and societal functioning. *American Psychologist, 43*, 15–22.

Sarbin, Theodore R. (Ed.). (1986). *Narrative psychology: The storied nature of human conduct*. New York: Praeger.

Schiebinger, Londa. (1989). *The mind has no sex? Women in the origins of modern science*. Cambridge, MA: Harvard University Press.

Schuster, Charles I. (1991). Theory and practice. In Erika Lindemann & Gary Tate (Eds.), *An introduction to composition studies* (pp. 33–48). New York: Oxford University Press.

Scott, Patrick. (1991). Bibliographical resources and problems. In Erika Lindemann & Gary Tate (Eds.), *An introduction to composition studies* (pp. 72–93). New York: Oxford University Press.

Selfe, Cynthia L. (1985). An apprehensive writer composes. In Mike Rose (Ed.), *When a writer can't write: Studies in writer's block and other composing-process problems* (pp. 83–95). New York: Guilford.

Selfe, Cynthia L. (1989). *Creating a computer-supported writing facility: A blueprint for action*. Houghton, MI: Computers and Composition.

Selzer, Jack. (1990). Critical inquiry in a technical writing course. In Donald A. Daiker & Max Morenberg (Eds.), *The writing teacher as researcher: Essays in the theory and practice of class-based research* (pp. 188–218). Portsmouth, NH: Boynton/Cook.

Shaughnessy, Mina P. (1977). *Errors and expectations: A guide for the teacher of basic writing*. New York: Oxford University Press.

Shor, Ira. (1980). *Critical teaching and everyday life*. Boston: South End.

Sides, Charles H. (Ed.). (1989). *Technical and business communication: Bibliographic essays for teachers and corporate trainers*. Urbana, IL, and Washington, DC: National Council of Teachers of English, and Society for Technical Communication.

Simons, Herbert W. (Ed.). (1989). *Rhetoric in the human sciences*. London: Sage.

Skinner, B. F. (1948). *Walden two*. New York: Macmillan.

Skinner, B. F. (1977). Herrnstein and the evolution of behaviorism. *American Psychologist, 32*, 1006–1012.

Skinner, B. F. (1983). *A matter of consequences: Part three of an autobiography*. New York: Knopf.

Slevin, James F. (1991). The politics of the profession. In Erika Lindemann & Gary Tate (Eds.), *An introduction to composition studies* (pp. 135–159). New York: Oxford University Press.

Smart, Graham. (1993). Genre as community invention: A central bank's response to its executives' expectations as readers. In Rachel Spilka (Ed.), *Writing in the workplace: New research perspectives* (pp. 124–140). Carbondale and Edwardsville: Southern Illinois University Press.

Smith, Laurence D. (1990). Metaphors of knowledge and behavior in the behaviorist tradition. In David E. Leary (Ed.), *Metaphors in the history of psychology* (pp. 239–266). Cambridge, MA: Cambridge University Press.

Sommers, Nancy. (1982). Responding to student writing. *College Composition and Communication, 33*, 148–156.

Spence, Donald P. (1982). *Narrative truth and historical truth: Meaning and interpretation in psychoanalysis*. New York: Norton.

Spilka, Rachel. (1988). Studying writer–reader interactions in the workplace. *The Technical Writing Teacher, 15*, 208–221.

Spilka, Rachel (Ed.). (1993). *Writing in the workplace: New research perspectives*. Carbondale and Edwardsville: Southern Illinois University Press.

Sprat, Thomas. (1959). *History of the Royal Society* (Jackson I. Cope & Harold W. Jones, Eds.). St. Louis, MO: Washington University Studies. (Original work published 1667)

Staats, Arthur W. (1991). Unified positivism and unification psychology: Fad or new field? *American Psychologist, 46*, 899–912.

Starker, Steven. (1989). *Oracle at the supermarket: The American preoccupation with self-help books*. New Brunswick, NJ: Transaction Publishers.

Sternberg, Robert J. (1988). *The psychologist's companion: A guide to scientific writing for students and researchers* (2nd ed.). Cambridge, England: Cambridge University Press.

Stoddart, Rebecca M., & Loux, Ann Kimble. (1992). And, not but: Moving from monologue to dialogue in introductory psychology/English writing courses. *Teaching of Psychology, 19*, 145–149.

Strenski, Ellen. (1989). Disciplines and communities, "armies" and "monasteries," and the teaching of composition. *Rhetoric Review, 8*, 137–145.

Stringer, Peter. (1990). Prefacing social psychology: A textbook example. In Ian Parker & John Shotter (Eds.), *Deconstructing social psychology* (pp. 17–32). London and New York: Routledge.

Strunk, William, Jr., & White, E. B. (1979). *The elements of style* (3rd ed.). New York: Macmillan.

Sutherland, James R. (1957). *On English prose*. Toronto: University of Toronto Press.

Swales, John M. (1990). *Genre analysis: English in academic and research settings*. Cambridge, England: Cambridge University Press.

Swift, Jonathan. (1962). *Gulliver's travels and other writings* (Miriam Kosh Starkman, Ed.). New York: Bantam Books. (Original work published 1735)

Tedesco, Janis. (1991). Women's ways of knowing/women's ways of composing. *Rhetoric Review, 9*, 246–256.

Thorngate, Warren. (1990). The economy of attention and the development of psychology. *Canadian Psychology, 31*, 262–271.

Tompkins, Jane. (1987). Me and my shadow. *New Literary History, 19*, 169–178.

Tompkins, Jane. (1988). Fighting words: Unlearning to write the critical essay. *Georgia Review, 42*, 585–590.

Trimbur, John. (1985). Collaborative learning and teaching writing. In Ben W. McClelland & Timothy R. Donovan (Eds.), *Perspectives on research and scholarship in composition* (pp. 87–109). New York: Modern Language Association.

Trimbur, John. (1989). Consensus and difference in collaborative learning. *College English, 51*, 602–616.

Trimbur, John. (1990). John Trimbur responds. *College English, 52*, 696–700.

Turabian, Kate L. (1987). *A manual for writers of term papers, theses, and dissertations* (5th ed.). Chicago and London: University of Chicago Press.

Tyson-Bernstein, Harriet. (1988). The academy's contribution to the impoverishment of America's textbooks. *Phi Delta Kappan, 70*(3), 192–198.

Unger, Rhoda K. (1989a). Introduction. In Rhoda K. Unger (Ed.), *Representations: Social constructions of gender* (pp. 1–11). Amityville, NY: Baywood.

Unger, Rhoda K. (Ed.). (1989b). *Representations: Social constructions of gender*. Amityville, NY: Baywood.

Valencia, Richard R. (1992a). The Cohen et al. responses: A new low in scholarship. *Contemporary Psychology, 37*, 505–506.

Valencia, Richard R. (1992b). Sticks 'n stones . . . *Contemporary Psychology, 37*, 504–505.

Varnum, Robin. (1992). The history of composition: Reclaiming our lost generations. *Journal of Advanced Composition, 12*, 39–55.

Vipond, Douglas. (1993). Social motives for writing psychology: Writing for and with younger readers. *Teaching of Psychology, 20*, 89–93.

Vipond, Douglas, & Hunt, Russell A. (1984). Point-driven understanding: Pragmatic and cognitive dimensions of literary reading. *Poetics, 13*, 261–277.

Vipond, Douglas, & Hunt, Russell A. (1991). The strange case of the queen-post truss: John McPhee on writing and reading. *College Composition and Communication, 42*, 200–210.

Vitz, Paul C. (1990). The use of stories in moral development: New psychological reasons for an old education method. *American Psychologist, 45*, 709–720.

Voss, Ralph F. (1983). Janet Emig's *The composing processes of twelfth graders*: A reassessment. *College Composition and Communication, 34*, 278–283.

Walsh-Bowers, Richard. (1992). The reporting and ethics of the research relationship in modern interpersonal psychology. Manuscript submitted for publication.

Walvoord, Barbara E., & McCarthy, Lucille P. (1990). *Thinking and writing in college: A naturalistic study of students in four disciplines.* Urbana, IL: National Council of Teachers of English.

Weaver, Richard M. (1953). *The ethics of rhetoric.* Chicago: Henry Regnery.

White, Murray J. (1983). Prominent publications in cognitive psychology. *Memory & Cognition, 11*, 423–427.

White, Murray J. (1987). Big bangs in perception: The most often cited authors and publications. *Bulletin of the Psychonomic Society, 25*, 458–461.

Winsor, Dorothy A. (1989). An engineer's writing and the corporate construction of knowledge. *Written Communication, 6*, 270–285.

Winsor, Dorothy A. (1990). Engineering writing/writing engineering. *College Composition and Communication, 41*, 58–70.

Wittrock, M. C., & Farley, Frank. (1992). The old educational psychology reviews the new. *Contemporary Psychology, 37*, 963–964.

Wresch, William (Ed.). (1991). *The English classroom in the computer age: Thirty lesson plans.* Urbana, IL: National Council of Teachers of English.

Young, Art. (1990). Storytelling in a technical writing class: Classroom-based research and community. In Donald A. Daiker & Max Morenberg (Eds.), *The writing teacher as researcher: Essays in the theory and practice of class-based research* (pp. 168–187). Portsmouth, NH: Boynton/Cook.

Young, Art, & Fulwiler, Toby (Eds.). (1986). *Writing across the disciplines: Research into practice.* Upper Montclair, NJ: Boynton/Cook.

Young, Richard E. (1978). Paradigms and problems: Needed research in rhetorical invention. In Charles R. Cooper & Lee Odell (Eds.), *Research on composing: Points of departure* (pp. 29–47). Urbana, IL: National Council of Teachers of English.

Young, Richard E., Becker, Alton L., & Pike, Kenneth L. (1970). *Rhetoric: Discovery and change.* San Diego: Harcourt Brace Jovanovich.

Zappen, James P. (1989). Francis Bacon and the historiography of scientific rhetoric. *Rhetoric Review, 8*, 74–88.

Zeiger, William. (1985). The exploratory essay: Enfranchising the spirit of inquiry in college composition. *College English, 47*, 454–466.

Zoellner, Robert. (1969). Talk-write: A behavioral pedagogy for composition. *College English, 30*, 267–320.

Index

About the Author

DOUGLAS VIPOND is Professor of Psychology at St. Thomas University (Fredericton, Canada). His articles on writing, reading and pedagogy have been published in journals such as *College Composition and Communication*, *Poetics*, and *Teaching of Psychology*.